Women in Power

Author
Sheila A. Taylor-Downer

Cover Design
Sandra Gorney – sgorney@speakeasy.net

Editor
Cheri R. Cox – cox32017@hotmail.com

ISBN: 0-9702909-1-8

Published by
Professional Prodigy Inc.
P. O. Box 641, Hillside, Illinois 60162-0641
Ph: 708.449.8058 ◆ Fax: 708.449.7858
website: www.professionalprodigy.com
email: professionalprodigy@yahoo.com

Copyright © 2003 by Professional Prodigy, Inc.
All rights reserved.

Except as permitted under the United States Copyright Act of 1976, no part of this publication may be reproduced, distributed, stored in any database or retrieval system, or transmitted in any form by any means, electronic, photo copying, reordering, scanning, without the prior written permission of the publisher.

POWERFUL

TALENTED

PASSIONATE

COURAGEOUS

Amazing Women

Acknowledgements

I want to thank and acknowledge those who have helped me, either in the completion of this book or supporting my workshops.

I would like to give a special thanks to my family and friends; Eugene Taylor, James Taylor, Sandra Taylor, Sharon Taylor, Schleria Taylor, Sherita Taylor, Chandra Taylor, Amania Drane, Angeley Johnson, Aretha Card, Beverly McKinley, Carolyn Curse (Sales & Marketing Queen), Cheri Cox (Editor), Christine Finley, David Tarlow, Erin Bowler, Jean Siwicki, Karen Coleman, Karen Lucas, Lois White, Margarita Gonzalez, Mary Keough, Molly Miller, Nichole Shields, Pamela McClay, Patricia Austin, Paula Villanueva, Phyllis Richardson, Roxanne Jackson (Motivational Guru), Shari Wenker (Mentor), Susan Rosen, Wendy Lumpkins, and especially Robyn Williams (writer extraordinaire).

Special Dedication

To all the women warriors who are fighting the war for freedom in Iraq; I salute you. But a special recognition goes out to my twin sister SGT. Sharon Taylor of the 416th Encom division who is serving in Kuwait — **YOU ARE MY HERO**.

Dedication

To my best friend and mother, Beatrice Taylor, who showed me how to be a woman in power.

My husband, Jerry Downer and last but not least, my twin daughters, BreAnna and Brittany Downer – You are the focus of my life!

Table of Content

Preface i

Dawn Cooper 1

Sheila A. Taylor-Downer (Author) 7

Amania Drane 17

Carol Hutchins 23

Senator Kimberly A. Lightford 31

Carla LeVeaux-Maiden 39

DeAnna M. McLeary & 45

Tiffanie N. McLeary 45

Wendy Lumpkins 53

Reverend Hattie Paulk 63

Hedy Ratner 73

Nilsa Reyna 81

Alice Faye Katrina Rodriguez 91

Susan Rosen 101

Mary Smith 109

Bonnie Ilyse Tunick 119

Nicole L. Wade 127

Caprice Wallace 135

Lois White 143

Robyn Williams 151

Thoughts &Reflections 157

Resources 167

Preface

Most women know what they want out of life or have an idea of what it is they wish to achieve. The challenge lies in bringing those hopes, dreams, and aspirations to fulfillment.

As a woman who constantly balances family needs versus my individual needs, I know all too well the difficulties of obtaining one's goals.

I understand that dedication and commitment are necessary tools to bring our goals to fruition. Experience has taught me that barriers are undoubtedly put before us to challenge or hinder us from actualizing our goals. However, despite innumerable and insurmountable odds, women are reaching and obtaining their goals far beyond our imagination. It is for this reason that I write this compelling book about *Women In Power*.

This extraordinary work brings to life the insightful and invigorating accounts of the triumphs and defeats of women who've claimed success as their destiny. These dynamic women personify greatness because they understand the maxim that failure is often fundamental to navigating the pathways to success.

These women are successful because they're starting their own businesses at twice the rate of men, thereby becoming major forces in the global marketplace. They are successful because they're rapidly climbing Corporate America's ladders despite exclusion from the good ole boys' networking concept. They

Preface

are successful because they are leaders who refuse to accept defeat!

Common triumphant threads underlie the stories vividly portrayed in *Women In Power*, claim them as your own. For these are your stories: stories reflective of women like you – women who have or will encounter similar situations yet refuse to give up!

Get ready to transform your personal dreams and visions into a victorious reality! Through these exciting and illuminating narratives you will become empowered. You are sure to value and grow from the hardships and emotional pain that the women herein have experienced. And you will laugh as you find out how they have effectively and creatively handled many of their challenges. *Women In Power* will enable you, the reader, to discover how when faced with the threat of trials and tribulations, you too can succeed! Just as the women whose stories shared herein have found success, *Women In Power* will certainly guide you in achieving the success, wealth, and happiness you so richly deserve!

*We are Courageous! We are Powerful!
We are Amazing Women!*

Dawn Cooper

Dawn Cooper

Another day at the office arrived and I had just interviewed another candidate for our customer service position. This gentleman had on a shiny cream shirt, cream pants and shiny cream shoes. I don't remember his resume, and, if I remember correctly, his answers were less than stellar. I left my office and said to one of my team members, "These folks are just not ready. I should start a business training them how to interview. That sounds too easy, huh?" She looked at me and said, "You sure should". I finished my day, never knowing that less than one year after making that statement, it would become a reality.

June 29, 2002…the day that changed my life. The entire division of wireless was closing and the recruitment department, myself included, was the first to go. Fortunately for me, God's divine power had been working in me a few months prior to that date and Career Link, Inc., the company "Connecting You to a Brighter Future" had already taken shape. I had started to write my business plan and had taken a course at Malcolm X College on how to start a successful business. Because my steps had been ordered, my soul cried out, "Hallelujah!" I was free at last.

Dawn Cooper

Although my original intent was to train people at interviewing, I began by preparing resumes for the people at my old company who would also be terminated. I thought to myself, "Well I might as well start making money right here in my own backyard". I made flyers and passed them out to everyone I knew and started doing resumes from my office, but eventually that segment of the market became dry. One day I said to myself, "Dawn, remember your focus. You want to train, resumes are secondary."

With that in mind, I remembered that I had compiled a list of contacts during my tenure as recruitment manager. As I sat under the dryer in my house, I began to go down that list and started calling, trying to find out when their job fairs were. My intention was to go to the job fairs, drum up interest in my programs, find a location to train and sign folks up for classes. NOT THE BEST IDEA. The initial contact was too short, finding a reasonable location was not easy, and the student commitment was too low. My method had to change.

One name on that list was worth mentioning. A job developer for the Center for Employment Training steered me in the right direction. He told me of different ways to drum up business and provided me with at least 5 references. Staying prayerful and committed to what I wanted to do; I set out to contact everyone he gave to me. Many said, "No thank you", some said, "We do the same thing" and some said, "Come meet with me." There were, and still are, days when I ask myself, "Dawn, what are you going to do if this does not work?" I would quickly erase that thought from my mind and say, "Anything works, if you work hard at it". Fortunately, God has also placed tremendous mentors and supporters in my life who have encouraged me to go on when the struggles seem too hard and begin to discourage me. But I am thankful for people like Leslie, a young lady who has owned an Allstate Agency for 10 years. She was a great mentor when I first started and told me to keep going, no matter what. Darrell, my accountant, also came into my life when I was getting started. When I first met with him I was so naïve. I was excited because I had met with Jesse Jackson, Sr. and he had gotten me in contact with one of his key people to discuss my programs. I just knew that this contact was going to come through and I would be set, just like getting a regular job. He asked me, "How long have you been doing this?" I said, "Just a couple of months". His expression said it all. He felt as though I needed more time invested into my company. We spoke at length about my goal and vision. He offered great advice, stating that I should not get discouraged, nor give up when things seem difficult. He stated that even if I lost one client, two or three would come behind them, and eventually, it would work itself out". I didn't quite see that then, but I do now. I use to get discourage in the beginning, but now I would sit and say, "This is my livelihood. Who knows what the future holds."

As I am now officially coming up on my 9th month in business, I celebrate the following accomplishments:

- I have learned how to effectively write and deliver a proposal

- I have expanded my programs from interviewing only. I now offer four classes; Interviewing, Resume Writing, Business Etiquette and Understanding Corporate Culture

- I have successfully trained at the high school level, in the welfare to work program scenario and at the college level

Dawn Cooper

- I have learned the real power of the pen…get it ALL in writing

- I have experienced the wonderful feeling of having a check made out to MY COMPANY, and

- I have grown in my faith in God and in the power of following the steps that He orders.

The Man Who Thinks He Can

If you think you are beaten, you are;
If you think you dare not, you don't.
If you'd like to win, but think you can't
It's almost a cinch you won't.
If you think you'll lose, you've lost,
For out in the world we find
Success begins with a fellow's will;
It's all in the state of mind.

If you think you're outclassed, you are:
You've got to think high to rise.
You've got to be sure of yourself before
You can ever win a prize.
Life's battles don't always go
To the stronger or faster man,
But sooner or later the man who wins
Is the man who thinks he can.

Author Unknown

Sheila Taylor-Downer

Women In Power

Sheila A. Taylor-Downer *(Author)*

As a teenager, I was determined to go to law school and set up my own practice. Entrepreneurship was my desire, my passion. I really enjoyed the legal field and helping others, but almost 15 years ago my dreams changed.

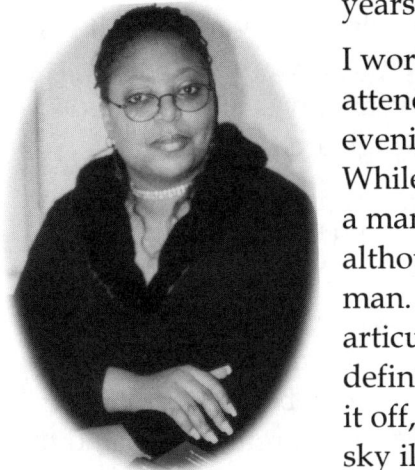

I worked full-time in the day and attended Roosevelt University in the evening, majoring in Business Law. While driving home one evening, I met a man we'll call Van. Several traits, although physical, attracted me to this man. He was tall, brown-skinned, articulate, and fashionably dressed – definitely not bad on the eyes. To top it off, the evening was perfect and the sky illuminated with stars.

The conversation was great! We exchanged numbers and he called the very next day. From the beginning, Van appeared genuine, kind, a true gentle being. He had so many notable qualities that when he asked if he could pick me up from school at night, I trusted him to keep me safe. He would call me every morning to make sure that I arrived to work on time. He would open doors and pull out my chair at restaurants. He was a true gentleman.

We attended many events together and immensely enjoyed each other's company. He was the answer to every mother's dream, the prince charming to every woman's fantasy — or so I thought. Van turned out to be my worst nightmare! How did I not see the signs? He always wanted to pick me up at night, denying my girlfriends a ride home, and he consistently critiqued my clothing. I realized then that Van was possessive and a little controlling. Although I was a bit concerned about these new "qualities" Van revealed — I ignored the signs. I believed that he sincerely cared about me and had my best interests at heart.

After dating for two months, Van thought it necessary to take our relationship to another level. At 21 years old, I was not ready for the next level or anything else. But Van made it very clear that I was no longer in my league, I was now playing with the "big boys." He was nine years my senior and his family is well connected in the Chicago area.

One day with a smile on his face, he jokingly stated that he would kill me if I tried to leave him. I didn't see the humor in that statement. The more I attempted to move on, the more controlling he became. He would stop by my house without calling and on several occasions escorted my girlfriends to the door, involuntarily. This prompted me to become frightened by Van and I realized that his goal was to promote fear and to exercise his need for power and control. Shortly thereafter, he hurt me. I guess I still find it hard to say that he raped me. Being raped is a horrendous and traumatizing experience. It's difficult to comprehend how someone can care so much for you and then commit such a violent act on your person. But I had to learn that **rape is about power, control, and anger, not romance and passion**. After the attack, Van called the next morning. I was so confused. I just wanted to know why he chose me? What did I do to cause this situation?

Van explained that he was only calling to inform me that he was moving on, that he could not afford to have a woman crying rape. Wasn't that a joke! But in a way, I was relieved. My words forced him to walk away. In the meantime, I tried to convince myself that this was a journey I had to travel. But deep down inside, I knew that his actions would scar me for life.

As time passed, it became apparent that I could no longer deal with the stress or the ordeal of being raped. I retreated to a dark place. I experienced bouts of depression and anger, feeling empty and ashamed. I had lost my self-respect, my dignity, my sense of pride and my freedom. I could no longer trust anyone, nor my own judgment. I blamed myself for what Van had done – convincing myself that I was responsible for his actions.

Feeling confused and ashamed, I thought; Who can I talk to? How can I speak the unspeakable? How can I face my friends, my family members and my schoolmates? Would they think that I asked for it? I knew that I would be judged unfairly which only contributed to feelings of insecurity. I tried to return to school and block out what happened, but I couldn't and my grades suffered. How could one innocent meeting turn my entire world upside down?

I began to question God. I could not fathom why He would permit such an atrocity to happen. What had I done to merit this? Eventually, the pressure was too much. I left school and became withdrawn. I purchased bars for my house and changed my appearance by cutting my hair. My inability to cope with my feelings led to food for comfort and the battle with obesity began! To make matters worst, Van decided to visit me six months after the incident. He had the audacity to knock on my door! I refused to open the door but allowed him to speak through the bars. He spoke as though he was sincerely sorry about what happened. But then, to add insult to injury, Van pointed out how I had taken on the "boy" look referring to my haircut and shapeless form. Even though I hated him – his words hit home. What had I done to myself?

I tried to erase the damage that I had done. I went on diets that did not work, joined health clubs that I did not attend, and spent money that I did not have on countless quick weight-loss programs. Nothing worked. I continued my path of destruction to lose weight and became bulimic.

Feeling worthless and depressed, I put all my dreams and aspirations on hold. I confined myself to a small space called the workplace and never looked back. I allowed fear to consume me, afraid that I would make the same mistake again.

Most believe that fear is a difficult emotion to describe. Well, I believe that I can describe it with just one word – imprisonment. I was so unhappy. I hated my job. I disliked my so-called friends. I despised what I had become – bitter and fat. The only comfort I had was food. But I knew that this was not the life for me.

After many pity parties, I decided to break the chain of destruction. I sought out a therapist to help me recover and rebuild my life. A close family member asked if I thought that I was crazy. I told her no. This was the sanest decision I had made for me in a long time. I also found emotional support from women who were fighting the same battles. I even joined overeater anonymous, feeling a need to be with others who were fighting the same demons. You see, sometimes we need more than what our family and friends can provide. I needed to learn how to nurture myself, relieve stress, and find rewards other than food. After much therapy and soul searching, I was finally on my way to healing.

It took many years to recover from the attack and on my journey back to finding myself, I made some horrible mistakes, but through it all, I learned to forgive myself. I finally met a man who became my best friend; John Whitaker. He understood my feelings and did not condemn me for my past.

He told me good things about myself and brought me inspirational books by Susan Taylor of **Essence** magazine. Cards, letters and articles were sent about healing the spirit. He helped me to believe that I was more than what I saw in the mirror. He said those most important words, "It wasn't your fault." His friendship was exactly what I needed, a friend who could deal with my mood swings and depression without judgment. John is and will always be a good friend of mine. He taught me one valuable lesson: that when I was being attacked, God did not give up on me, it was then that He spared my life. He also shared a poem with me that I will always cherish and keep dear to my heart - Footprints in the Sand, which portrays the lesson that God embraces and brings you through your circumstances.

Footprints in the Sand

Last night I had a dream. I dreamed I was walking along the beach with the Lord. Across the sky flashed scenes from my life. For each scene, I noticed two sets of footprints in the sand: one belonged to me, the other to the Lord.

After the last scene of my life flashed before me, I looked back at the footprints in the sand. I noticed that at many times along the path of my life, especially at the very lowest and saddest times, there was only one set of footprints.

This really troubled me, so I asked the Lord about it. "Lord, you said once I decided to follow you, You'd walk with me all the way. But I noticed that during the saddest and most troublesome times of my life, there was only one set of footprints. I don't understand why, when I needed You the most, You would leave me."

The Lord replied, "My child, my precious child, I love you and I would never leave you. During your times of suffering, when you could see only one set of footprints, it was then that I carried you."

Author Unknown

Lesson learned

Rape is not an act of passion. It is a violent crime punishable by law. Rape does not discriminate. Age, race, religion, sex or size does not matter. Victims are not chosen because of the way they look or what they wear, rather because of their vulnerability or the attacker's opportunity. No one deserves to be raped!

I tell this story not to sadden you but to encourage you to fight even in the face of adversity. Keep in mind, there are others who have faced many trials and tribulations and have endured tremendous pain and suffering, but they did not give up. In truth, it is not how hard you fall - but how you rise to the occasion!

Even though at times I am haunted by my past, I will never allow another to steal my power, to determine my future or to validate my worth. I pledge to face my fears head-on. And now due to BreAnna and Brittany, I undoubtedly know that there is more beauty in this world then ugliness.

I returned to school and received an Associate of Arts in Business Administration. I conduct seminars and workshops, teaching and training on economic empowerment. How ironic, I was once reclusive and now I am a motivational speaker empowering other women not to accept defeat. Teaching them that barriers are undoubtedly put before us to challenge or hinder us from actualizing our goals. However, despite innumerable and insurmountable odds, we can reach goals beyond imagination. My plans were slightly altered but I still brought my dreams of being an entrepreneur to fruition. I am an Entrepreneur teaching other Entrepreneurs how to fulfill their dreams. What could be better?

Currently, I am married to a wonderful and kind-hearted man name Jerry. I am also the mother of a set of beautiful, exceptional twin girls, BreAnna and Brittany. I know that I made a good decision when it comes to my marriage and family. I know this because everything about it feels right.

For more than a decade, I have wondered why it has taken so long to arrive at a place where I feel good about my choices. But in spite of how long it took, I am glad to finally be in a place where I can look back and know that the choices I made were right for me.

P.S. I'm still overweight, but I'm happy ☺.

Biography

Sheila is a native Chicagoan and attended Roosevelt University in Chicago. She has an Associate of Arts in Business Administration. She is a small business development advisor and a job developer. She founded Professional Prodigy Inc. (PPI) in January of 1997, with the belief that she could make a difference. She has instructed and spoken at many workshops and seminars on personal development through education and training for both career opportunities and entrepreneurship.

Sheila teaches with passion; and is dynamic and enthusiastic. She delivers a motivational and inspirational message on

Sheila Taylor-Downer

economic empowerment to audiences throughout the United States. Her mission is to Promote, Educate, Empower and Raise Awareness on the subject of Entrepreneurship. She states "In order to be successful you must become innovative or become a thing of the past. In these volatile and uncertain, economic times, innovation and imagination are essential to survival."

Sheila is a motivational speaker that you won't soon forget. She received a Who's Who In America award in 1999. She has spoken at many empowerment seminars and workshops and served on several self-publishing panels. She appeared on WVON's Radio Station "Movers and Shakers" and was recognized by the Proviso-Leyden Council for Community Action, Inc. for forging a partnership with Anna Marie Sloan of American Mailers. That partnership helped to place more than 80 local residents in long-term employment. In March of 2003, the Chicago Defender featured her firm because she is able to create a plan of long-term economic stability.

Because Sheila recognizes that education and training is a vital part of the community and is the key to success, she has created a series of workshops for entrepreneurs and business professionals. She also believes if you are employed today, be prepared for the day you're not.

For more information contact Professional Prodigy, Inc. at (708) 449-8058.

Email: professprodigy@aol.com

Amania Drane

Women In Power

Amania Drane

In the spring of 1992, I changed my name from "Anita Drane" to "Amania Anita Drane". "Amania" is Swahili meaning "Trust with Confidence." I didn't start off that February of 1992 even thinking about changing my name, but when asked to assist with an African Name-Changing Program at St. Stephen Baptist Church in Louisville, KY, I guess it became more than just a notion.

I had returned from Africa in 1990 and the experience had been life changing. Upon my return to the U.S., I recall working, encouraging, and learning from others in the church about African culture. It was a time of a lot of soul-searching. I struggled with my "Afro centricity" and also with my understanding of certain teachings of the church. I still loved learning the "Word" and was very involved in church activities. I had a firm belief in God's presence and power. It was just a lot of other "religious stuff" that I was fraught with.

Well, one February night while taking a shower, it just "hit" me. I was so busy sharing my experiences in Africa with others that I hadn't even thought about taking on an African name for myself! I had no idea what I wanted my new name to be, but I knew the meaning had to be something based on my faith in God. Oh yes, I had my doubts and still do. But I never doubted the existence of God and God's love for me or for all people. I needed a name that exemplified no matter how much doubt I struggled with, I would always hold onto my faith and belief in God. A name that gave me strength and was like a rock—like that large, heavy rock that's deep inside a pitch-dark cave. I needed a name that regardless of what I went through in life, I would be determined to hold onto "God's unchanging hand." It would be my solid rock. Regardless of how deep I went into the world and experienced new and different things, that rock, that name, would be my foundation.

A few weeks later, I met with my sister and some friends and we started discussing African names. As soon as "Amania" was read from an African dictionary, I knew that was it! I called my mother that night and told her. The first thing she said was "Wait." She left the phone for a brief minute and then came back. I asked her what she was doing. She said she wanted to write it in her Bible. At that instant, I experienced my "name adding ceremony."

Since that experience, I've been in many different pitch-dark caves. For me, that hasn't always been so bad. Sometimes experiencing a dark cave can give you time to rest, time to learn about yourself, and a little peace of mind. It gives you time to "be still and know."

In my life, I have visited a couple of those caves. There's the "Comfortable where you are" cave. While in college, I spent so much time working, hanging out with friends, being involved in everything, that it left very little time for school. It was a struggle and one day a friend said to me "Anita, you don't have to push yourself so hard. It's o.k. if you don't finish school." This was a friend who saw how much I was struggling in school and wanted me to know that our friendship was more than me proving I could obtain a college degree. I appreciate that friend's love and acceptance, but in life, if you don't get your priorities straight, there are a lot of things you won't be able to do.

Then there is the "Grieving" cave. It was October 1997 when my mother "passed on." Wow, you talk about the importance of grieving! I was away from many of my friends and family, living in Chicago. My job was really stressful, and I just didn't have the joy and the laughter that once was a part of me.

A dear friend was visiting from out of town and noticed I wasn't the same "Anita/Amania" she had known for many years. I talked about work and how stressed I was. She said, "it's o.k. to quit your job if things have gotten too hard. Maybe this just isn't for you." You see, sometimes when life gets really hard and people tell you it's o.k. to not work so hard, to not try so hard to push yourself—it is then that you should pray. Ask God to give you direction. With many mixed emotions; I just wanted to quit, go home to Kentucky and live in the house where my mother had lived and spend more time with my family and friends. But the answer is never to quit. It was then that I understood how saying my name and calling on the Lord would help me. It gave me confidence to say "Amania"! You see when things seem overwhelming, it's then that you've got to step back and re-evaluate the situation. Ask yourself: Is it really too hard? Or can you endure it little longer?

Then there is the "Robbin' Peter to pay Paul" cave. Oh, been to this cave several times. It's when you get the credit cards for the first time and you want to go out to treat yourself and all your friends (show-off) and you think it's only $5.00 a month on your credit card. Well, you tend to forget it's another $5.00 a month every time you go on one of your shopping sprees, and you've been on quite a few. They start adding up and before you know it, you're using credit to pay bills, and it just becomes a vicious cycle. I've visited that cave way too many times, and I'm not going back there.

Well, things got better. I endured a little longer, worked a little harder and then finally received my Bachelor's Degree in 1990 from the University of Louisville. I endured and finally got through that extremely stressful time at work and now truly love getting up in the morning and going to work! I've even left the "Grieving" cave. A friend once said, "your mom is in a better place, and even if she could come back, she wouldn't." What peace and joy that gives me! When I get sad and start missing Momma, I think about the good times we had. I think about the 62 years of her life that she was blessed to be here. I think of her kindness. I think about her tucking me in bed at night even when I was much too old to be tucked in by anybody. I think about us taking walks in the country.

I've visited many caves in my life and I'm sure I'll go to many more. But the strength I receive from being Amania, the Lord's unwavering hand, and the "Trust with Confidence" rock is what will get me through those hard times.

Professional

Amania Drane is currently a Human Resources Representative at State Farm Insurance Companies in Elmhurst, IL. She is also the owner of Nia Enterprises, an event planning and real estate investment company. She is currently pursuing a Masters in Management & Organizational Behavior at Benedictine University.

Email: niaenterprises@peoplepc.com

Carol Hutchins

Best wishes, Karyn!
warmly,
Carol

Women In Power

Carol Hutchins

The pain of my own childhood bullying experience instantly came revisiting the day my daughter came home in tears from her first day in kindergarten. I listened to my dear Ellie talk of kids teasing about her lisp, her crooked teeth and the gangling movements she had on the playground. "Scarface!" "Al Capone!" The words, now 40 years old, crashed inside me as if a bowling alley had been installed in my head. How could they not see past her "duckling" stage and notice the unfolding beauty of her enduring kindness and gentle spirit? Her tears flowed…my heart slowed.

My first reaction raced to the motherly protective mode, then darted to the over-reacting lunatic and finally, to the voice of reason. I took a very long, deep breath…remembering once again the desperation of wanting an understanding and attentive ear. Breathe. Now my thoughts turned to my daughters need. What kind of lifeline could I throw her? Eyes closed and imagining being in her shoes, what was she feeling? What would she want me to say or maybe even not say to her at this moment? Inability to talk about my situation prevented anyone from knowing how deep the hurt had gone. I felt my story had disappeared over the years. The challenge at this special moment was for history to not repeat itself.

Carol Hutchins

I spent the first two years talking with Ellie's schoolteachers, the parents of the bullies and lots of friends. The teachers and friends had the same advice…tell her to just walk away. If you've ever been bullied, those are not the words you'd ever want to hear and more importantly, it doesn't work. "Scaredy-cat! Chicken! Mommy's' girl!" Those are the words you hear back using that futile technique. The parents of the bullies…a total state of denial. "It was a joke!" "My child would never do something like that!"

Attempting to emerge from the heap of injustice she was enduring, I longed to help Ellie learn the tools and skills she would need to become a self-confident, respectful and caring young lady. Already armed with a degree in Communication, along with my own life experience, I went back to school to become certified as a mediator. This was an opportunity to meld mediation, whose goal is to create win-win situations and communication strategies and awareness. The idea appealed to my sense of fairness and strength. Now it felt as if I'd been given a chance to redeem myself by finding practical and realistic ways for Ellie to handle the exact same issues.

Just as one would train for a competition to gain strength, proficiency, and knowledge of the game, Ellie and I began to practice life skills everyday. Communicating through letter writing was where we started. She could quickly see how her written words were a window into her broken heart. Her powerful words gave her energy. No matter about the epistles sent to her harassers and met with mixed reviews. The letters provided needed affirmation her feelings were real.

Walking. We practiced walking. Walking into a room with a purpose. "Hold your head up Ellie…breathe…fill the air with your presence!" So, she walked many times. Small and unworthy, Ellie entered the room. The impact of the teasing had taken such a hurtful toll on her young spirit. And yet, each baby step helped her to see how tall she could feel and as time passed her footsteps quickened. Like magic, she could glide in the room…light on her feet and wearing a petite, uncertain smile. Ellie was making progress.

Role-playing became our practice before game time. We brainstormed the variety of scenarios the "other team" would bring and then how to effectively and creatively handle each situation. Ellie played every part…beautifully, I might add. Offense. Defense. Coach. Cheerleader. Spectator. Referee. Unfolding in her growing mind was a new appreciation of what it's like to be in someone else's shoes and what motivates people to act and react in ways difficult to understand. Words like respect and empathy became part of a usual conversation between the two of us. She had gained so much strength, skills and strategies over the years, it was obvious the long talks, the hours of listening and the practice had paid off. Sometimes, I felt flickers of gratefulness that I was given so many teaching moments in her life.

One month into her freshman year of high school, I drove to school to give Ellie a ride home. This day, she hopped into the car… literally hopped into the car. I was astonished. "Mom, guess what?" My curiosity was leaping with the pounding of her heart. "I finally have friends!" The words hit me like a rock. The look on my face spoke for me. "Mom, that's good. It's really, really good! I finally have friends!" Her happiness and enthusiasm was positively catchy. I didn't allow the sadness I felt creep in. She had hit pay dirt and I was thrilled to be part of her success. For her, life's journey had just begun.

Who knew that "ride" would take me on a path of sharing our stories with so many? Together, we had learned much about bullies, their targets and the bystanders who witness such cruelty everyday. Soon, people were seeing the confidence and glow from Ellie's entire being. She had gotten her wings. Ellie became a peer mediator at school, an example to others in the classroom. Her fairness and gentleness elevated her status to one of kind respect.

Knowing we had successfully conquered one fragment in the trials and tribulations of childhood, I began teaching children how to communicate effectively, how to settle conflicts equitably, as well as, lessons of respect and empathy. I began small, on a volunteer basis…listening especially to the ones who had no voice. They came in all colors, sizes and shapes. As they shared their life stories, my task was to help them learn a common language of peace. Clearly, the time had come for a renewed faith in finding effective ways to communicate and put injustice to rest.

Teachers, parents, and administrators loved the inclusiveness of my lessons, using practical, meaningful and interesting methods. Soon, I was asked to teach the teachers, the parents, the community leaders, and those who influence the lives of our children. Our stories, Ellie and mine, rang true for so many. Now, the adult students had tools and skills and permission to tell their own life stories. And there was a sense for many, they could in turn lift up their own.

I'm convinced it's the way a good and worthy story should travel. One listens intently, draws similarities and differences, thinks thoughtfully about the words, becomes enlightened and then passes it along to share life lessons with another. So as Ellie heard my story, she realized she was not alone. And as I told her story, I realized I was not alone and that gives us lots of strength, and pride and a reason never to be silent again.

Women In Power

Email: TheKukla@aol.com

Intimidation

The new kid on the block; I'm considered green.
Though I possess more experience than the combined team.

They have no idea; my patience will win;
I've been down this road again and again.

I know their plan; keep me in my place.
Embarrass me at every moment; try to redden my face.

But I'll rise to the occasion, as I have in the past
I'll deflect their taunts with wisdom and class

Try me my friends; I'm strong you'll see.
Every hurting word cast just encourages me.

I believe in myself and my Maker believes in me.
So with His support I stand, never giving a degree.

It's really no use — give up now;
no matter how I'm bullied, I'll bounce back some how.

So yes I sit and I smile and I brush off rude remarks,
because my faith is rooted deep in my heart.

By Beverly McKinley

*Senator
Kimberly
Lightford*

Women In Power

Senator Kimberly A. Lightford

State Senator, 4th District

"I believe we must stand firm on the need for positive change and strengthened policies as we move forward in the 21st Century."

I never planned or expected to become a State Senator. It just seemed to happen. It was a blessing.

On January 8, 2003, I was sworn into my second term as Senator. I won by an overwhelming majority from the people of the 4th Senate District. I have accomplished a great deal in the short amount of time since I set foot in the Senate Chamber.

When I was elected in 1998, I was the youngest woman and the youngest African-American elected to the Illinois Senate. I have served as chair of the Illinois Senate Black Caucus since I was a freshman legislator.

I never thought I would be where I am today. I sort of stumbled upon this career. I was stopped at a neighborhood traffic light in Maywood in the winter of 1995, when I glanced out of my car window and noticed a boarded-up recreational park facility.

The Truth-In-Sentencing Act had just passed and one of the first young men affected by this law was from my community. It really disturbed me that our elected officials were closing up

Senator Kimberly Lightford

alternatives to the streets, such as a recreational center when stricter sentencing laws made them even more necessary.

After seeing the abandoned recreational park facility, I visited my State Representative, Eugene Moore, to discuss my concerns. He was upfront with me and asked if I was going to be a part of the problem or part of the solution. He encouraged me to become more involved in my hometown and suggested I run as a Trustee for the Village of Maywood.

During this time, I was an intern for the Illinois House Democrats during the 88th and 89th General Assemblies (1994 to 1996), where I was able to gain insight into the legislative process.

I not only gained experience in the state legislature as an intern, but I also gained experience in state government agencies. I received my undergraduate degree in Public Communication from Western Illinois University and a Master's Degree in Public Administration from the University of Illinois at Springfield. I gained extensive management experience working at the Illinois Department of Central Management Services, the Illinois Department of Corrections, the University of Illinois at Springfield, and the Illinois Secretary of State's office.

In 1997, I took my Springfield experiences home and decided to run for Maywood Village Trustee. I won my first election in April of that year when I was voted into one of the six open seats out of seventeen candidates.

During my tenure on the Village Board, 1997-2003, I championed my passion for youth development and became chair of the Recreation Youth and Senior Services Committee. I also was chair of the Advisory Council for the Boys & Girls Club.

Soon after I became a Trustee, word circulated in November of 1997 that the current State Senator from the 4th District, Earlean Collins, was planning to retire from the Illinois Senate. Recognizing my political potential, I was approached by Maywood Mayor Joe Frelon, State Representative Moore, and other community activists, to run in the upcoming primary.

I was flattered that these individuals thought I would be capable of running for such an honorable position. I was excited about the idea of running for the Illinois Senate, but I kept thinking that I was going to be facing six opponents during the primary. Two of the candidates had strong name recognition from previous primary elections, and they also had the support of a well-known Congressman.

Despite the odds, I decided to run for the position. My campaign consisted of my father, sister and two aunts who had worked in previous city elections. I focused primarily in the Proviso Township Area, where I was raised and graduated from Proviso East High School.

On March 17, 1998, I dominated in precincts that were neglected by other candidates. I also maintained enough of a percentage in areas, such as Oak Park and my district's Chicago West Side, to win the primary election and eventually be sworn in as the Honorable Kimberly A. Lightford.

It was an incredible feeling. It was a great accomplishment, not only to be elected once by the people of the 4th District, but also to be elected twice.

Senator Kimberly Lightford

When my predecessor retired early, I was sworn into office in November 1998.

During the 93rd General Assembly, I will continue my efforts to improve the quality of life for those within my district, as well as the people of Illinois. I serve as Chair of the Senate Financial Institutions Committee, and a member of the Education and State Government Committees. I will continue to co-chair the Commission on Intergovernmental Cooperation and continue to be active in my district serving on the Board of Directors for the Proviso-Leyden Council for Community Action, Inc. and Loretto Hospital. I am also a member of Delta Sigma Theta Sorority, Inc.

As a State Senator, I have sponsored legislation to improve public education and health care focusing on women issues and have helped low-income children to receive a hot breakfast while at school. In addition, I am proud to have sponsored legislation allowing working mother to have a private place at work to express milk for their babies.

I have championed the right of working families and believe that every family deserves the right to have adequate health care opportunities, as well as good pensions after they retire. In the future, I will fight to ensure my district receives its fair share of state funding.

In my leadership role, I am trying to pass legislation that is empowering to women in order to allow them to better themselves in their work environment as well as at home.

This job is hard work, and you have to be mindful in what you do and what you want to accomplish. It is truly rewarding and it gives you personal gratification.

Awards

Senator Lightford has received numerous awards during her tenure as a State Senator. Some of her awards include the Western Illinois University Alumni of the Year, the Legislative Leadership Award from the Illinois Alcoholism and Drug Dependence, Habilitative Systems, Inc.: "Freeing the Human Spirit" Award, the Chicago Teachers Union Certificate of Commendation for Support of Public Education (1999-2000), and an appreciation award from the School Based Health Center at Proviso East High School from Loyola Hospital.

It Is Not The Critic Who Counts

It is not the critic who counts, not the one who points out how the strong man stumbled or how the doer of deeds might have done better. The credit belongs to the man who is actually in the arena, whose face is marred with sweat and dust and blood; who strives valiantly; who errs and comes short again and again; who knows the great enthusiasms, the great devotions, and spends himself in a worthy cause; who, if he wins, knows the triumph of high achievement; and who, if he fails, at least fails while daring greatly, so that his place shall never be with those cold and timid souls who know neither victory or defeat.

By Theodore Roosevelt

Carla LeVeaux-Maiden

Women In Power

Carla LeVeaux-Maiden

In the fall of 1983, I was a young aspiring college student and I gave a speech on suicide. I can remember reflecting and saying that there wasn't any experience that would ever make me want to take my own life. However, at the same time, I thought, except if I was raped. At that moment in time, I didn't believe that I would want to live after experiencing such a horrible act. Fifteen years later my words were put to the test.

On February 14, 1998, I endured a horrific experience. It was just before midnight when I was awakened to violence and terror that would endure until daylight. My two precious children were asleep down the hall. I prayed and cried out to God to shield and protect them from awakening to the horror in their parent's room. As I begged him to stop and fought back, the more enraged and violent he became. I knew that the more I fought and refused him the worse off I would be and even worse; the children could awaken to this horror. I remember saying to myself how could I have let things get this bad. No matter how bad the relationship got he was my husband. I wanted him to stop and I pleaded and begged but to no avail. I was terrified at the anger that raged from him. This couldn't be the man I married. So many things ran through my mind; "Had I been such a bad wife to deserve such abuse? Dear God, why didn't I have the courage to leave before things got to this point?" I was experiencing so many mixed emotions; guilt, shame, anger, and extreme fear. I laid there trembling and petrified but I knew that I would have to pull myself together because the children would awaken soon. I could hide most of my bruises and scars, but I could not hide my blood shot eyes. When my husband left for church, I took the opportunity to call for help. I was so embarrassed by the whole incident that I couldn't bring myself to call my mom or dad. How could I explain to them what had happened to me? I called it a horrific experience because I couldn't admit to myself that I was raped. I needed help and I needed it fast. I was so overwhelmed with fear and I didn't know what to do. I could not accept this as being a way of life. I had to find inner strength and determination to take back what was stolen from me. I had lost my sense of safety and security. How can someone that is suppose to love you and protect you cause you so much pain and fear? I asked myself, would it have been better to be raped by a stranger. If it was a stranger would I have been victimized over and over again by loved ones and friends, who found it hard to believe me, talk to me, or even comfort me in my darkest hour.

I praised God through this trial as my faith and love for Christ was strengthened. One thing I realized during this battle to survive my assault was that God's love is unconditional, constant and everlasting. Even when I found it hard to love myself, God was never failing. I found my peace and security in knowing that I was worthy! Fear would not rule my life because I was protected by a much higher power My Lord and Savior Jesus Christ.

I knew the road ahead as a divorced corporate working mom was rough but the rewards were greater than I could have ever imagined at the time my journey began. I work for a top accounting firm and I am in a leadership position. I have grown closer to my children and we have spent more quality time together than we ever did before. I had to learn to trust others again and on May 24, 2002, I was blessed with a spirit-filled, loving and supportive husband.

Almost 20 years later, I can say from experience that there is life after rape.

The Key

There was a key to my heart given when it wasn't mine to give.

There was a love shared when it was forbidden by God to be shared.

There was a child conceived that never reached full life, because, it was conceived in sin our child paid the ultimate price.

Now it's time to put away the key that wasn't mine to give, and seek the Lord to mend and heal the damage to All Hearts.

by Carla LeVeaux-Maiden

DeAnna M.
&
Tiffanie N. McLeary

Women In Power

DeAnna M. McLeary &
Tiffanie N. McLeary

It was a typical hot muggy day in Tallahassee, Florida. I was working on my master thesis paper in anticipation of receiving my MBA in the coming weeks when I received a phone call from my sister who believed she had a great idea. Here she goes with her great ideas I thought silently. She expressed her interest in starting a magazine geared to young women of color. Her idea came about as she observed her African-American female 5th grade students consult **Seventeen Magazine** for hair, dress, and other lifestyle ideas. My sister empathized with her students, knowing she too consulted **Seventeen Magazine** as a young girl and felt they didn't quite focus on her specific needs as an African-American young woman. Thus, my sister perceived there was a strong need and a huge market for a "teen" magazine geared to women of color. I was extremely skeptical, my first thoughts were — this is a good idea but not very unique. I knew nothing about the publishing industry and wondered why this idea had not been capitalized

DeAnna M. McLeary & Tiffanie N. McLeary

upon in the past. My love for my sister prohibited me from discouraging her, even though I questioned her ability to start a magazine. With all this said my gut instinct was to use my business background to help my sister in every way possible. Today, my sister is Editor and I am the CEO of Melanin Inc., publishing house for **Melanin Magazine**.

It is significant in all ethnicities to display positive images that represent the average person. Our magazine is for the forgotten teen girl. The girl who doesn't see images of herself celebrated on television, in print, or even on her high school's cheerleading squad. **Melanin Magazine** is committed to becoming the first magazine publication specifically targeting the pre-teen to teenage young lady of color. Melanin aims to become the leader in "people of color publications," based both on circulation and advertising. Melanin strives to empower young women of color.

As mentioned, I was initially apprehensive about dedicating my time to something that seemed so risky. I let pessimistic thoughts run rampant in my mind. I began to worry about competitors, whether the market for young women of color was viable, and my ability to build a company. Thus, I began doubting myself before I had done any sort of groundwork. With much deliberation, my final decision was to follow my heart, to step out on faith, to believe in myself and trust my own abilities. My heart had spoken to me and I truly felt this was something I had to do. Life is about taking risks and I always told myself I would not follow the path of least resistance. My path of least resistance was extremely too comfy.

Several months after receiving my MBA, I was climbing the ranks at one of the largest consulting firms in the world. My salary was more than enough, and even though corporate America brought many stresses, I was learning a lot and rubbing elbows with many "important" people. However, I was not fulfilled and I knew my comfortable corporate job would not allow me to help the less fortunate in significant ways, which was a lifetime goal.

But, is corporate America really less risky than being a business owner? Factoring in the probability of corporate fraud and downsizing, an afterthought at one time, which is now becoming quite common. Is it more risky to put my life in other people's hands or in my own hands? Is it wise to invest majority of my time in a career that will yield minimal returns? Do I really want to live my whole life in the 9 to 5 rat race (consulting is a 7am to 10pm rat race)? Why can't the fruits of my labor bring me happiness? Why can't I have more flexibility in my day? Is this too much to ask? In essence, Melanin Inc. fit with several of my lifetime goals; joy, freedom, and being a blessing to others.

As a result, I stopped allowing life to push me around and I took control of my life. I refused to sit around and wait for opportunities to magically appear, I searched and created opportunities. I began to envision **Melanin Magazine** as a global publication. I wrote down all the possible people who could possibly help me and networked with these individuals. I researched and read books on magazine publishing. Someone once told me, "Opportunity is often missed, because it comes dressed in overalls and looks like work." Starting a business is a lot of work but only action brings potential to life and the rewards are immeasurable. So, I refused to make excuses and only allowed myself to think positive thoughts.

DeAnna M. McLeary & Tiffanie N. McLeary

The mind is powerful and your thoughts become your world. I began to dream BIG.

Even though we envision success, people doubted my sister and I. Many couldn't see our vision, and in some instances it was the people who loved us the most who discouraged us. This was mostly due to them not wanting to see us fail. But, success is the result of failing. The only true failure is not trying. It is important to not get side tracked by negative people. There are many dream killers out there. I treat my dreams like jewels; they don't get shared with everyone.

Melanin remains in the building phase and as of January 2003, we are on our 2nd issue. I am certain that **Melanin** will become a successful entity. My sister has sacrificed significantly, she has sold her house and invested the capital into Melanin, and I have left my corporate job. I am excited about the future, like a great quote says, "Success is a journey not a destination." I'm savoring the journey.

I have learned to listen to that voice inside of me. I always wanted to go into business for myself but never could think of my niche. It is a blessing my niche was revealed to me, and my inner voice kept saying, "This is it". My advise to women who are considering venturing out of their comfort zone to explore something new and exciting is to follow your heart, don't ignore your inner voice, and have courage. Rare is the courage to follow talent wherever it leads, strive to be one of those rare people. As one of my dearest friends once told me, "Everything in life becomes too hard at some point, so focus on doing the things you love, because the ones you hate will become a challenge too."

www.melaninmagazine.com

IF

If you can keep your head when all about you .. Are losing theirs and blaming it on you; If you can trust yourself when all men doubt you, .. But make allowance for their doubting too; If you can wait and not be tired by waiting .. Or, being lied about, don't deal in lies, Or, being hated, don't give way to hating, .. And yet don't look too good, nor talk to wise;

If you can dream - and not make dreams your master; If you can think - and not make thoughts your aim; If you can meet with triumph and disaster .. And treat those two impostors just the same;

If you can bear to hear the truth you've spoken
.. Twisted by knaves to make a trap for fools, Or watch the things you gave your life to broken, .. And stoop, and build 'em up with worn-out tools; If you can make one heap of all your winnings .. And risk it on one turn of pitch-and-toss, And lose, and start again at your beginnings .. And never breathe a word about your loss; If you can force your heart and nerve and sinew .. To serve your turn long after they are gone, And so hold on when there is nothing in you
.. Except the Will, which says to them: "Hold on!"

If you can talk with crowds and keep your virtue, .. Or walk with kings - nor lose the common touch; If neither foes nor loving friends can hurt you; .. If all men count with you, but none too much; If you can fill the unforgiving minute .. With

DeAnna M. McLeary & Tiffanie N. McLeary

sixty seconds' worth of distance run .. Yours is the Earth and everything that's in it, .. And - which is more - you'll be grown up my child!

Rudyard Kipling

Wendy Lumpkins

Wendy Lumpkins

"From Death to Life, I was reborn"

i am not a minister, evangelist, apostle or profit appointed by man nor am I representing a church. I am simply a fellow-servant of the Lord and your brethren doing what God told me to do. This is my story.

About ten years ago, I got a good paying receptionist job at a Chicago downtown accounting firm. While working there, I always had dreams of going into marketing and advertising but there was no way for a receptionist to ever make it to the top, especially without a degree. A few years later, I decided to go to college full-time and work there part-time. I was 25 years old with a great job, in college pursuing my dreams and dating the boyfriend I thought I would marry. I considered myself to be a good person. I liked everyone and I didn't have a jealous bone in my body. Moreover, if you asked me, I would give you the clothes off my back. I knew God and how to pray. I recited the Lord's Prayer and gave my life to Him in 1993. I thought I was being the best I could be and that was all that was required by me.

Working part-time and going to school every day was really wearing me down physically. I didn't take a lunch break; I only had a 15-minute morning break that I used for lunch. One summer Friday afternoon, I had to pay a couple of bills and pick up lunch all within my 15-minute break. Surprisingly, I was able to run to the phone company, the light company and pick up a burger from my favorite place.

Wendy Lumpkins

Getting back to work with all things accomplished, I felt great for a moment. Immediately after sitting down to eat, I became dizzy, violently nauseous, my sight became blurred and everything moved in slow motion. Not knowing what was happening to me; I quickly ran to my seat at the front desk and rested my head. My co-workers were very attentive but I couldn't tell them what was wrong with me because every time I opened my mouth, I would feel more nauseous. They advised me to lay my head at the rear security counter that would be closing in a few minutes. I didn't want to go home because I thought I would be just fine if I rested for a few minutes. My boyfriend was picking me up from work in a few hours and he would take me home. I laid there for some time, and then I fell into a deep sleep. I was asleep for about 2 hours when a security guard slammed his hand on the counter and yelled, "Wake up!", to get a laugh. Being awakened abruptly jumpstarted my nausea and began a series of uncontrollable stomach upset. I quickly ran down a long hallway to a secluded bathroom. It was there I had a death to life experience where I was severely dehydrated, comatose for 5 hours and had an out-of-body experience that changed my life.

While sick in the bathroom, I was sure that any one of my co-workers would come in the bathroom to check on me; the cleaning crew would find me or even security would make their usual rounds and get help. No one came. Hours of throwing up and passing out with no one looking for me was scary. "My boyfriend was picking me up from work....he'll find me", I kept telling myself. But nothing. No one came to look for me because no one knew where I was. I was alone and dying. I felt an incredible sleep come over me again. After what seemed like an eternity of rest, I was suddenly in complete darkness.

I was conscious of nothing but darkness. I kept looking around but I couldn't see anything. No light from anywhere. I tried putting my hands in front of my face, I tried running so I can bump into something and nothing was there. I was in vast darkness and it was getting cold. Not yet freezing but cool. I tried blowing my breath to see if I could see the condensation coming from my mouth but still nothing. I started to panic, thinking, where am I? How did I get here? Who put me here? Was I abducted? Is someone trying to kill me? I then tried to focus on the last thing I remembered. And in a flash, a vision came to existence. I saw a girl laying down in squalor. I couldn't see her face because her braids covered it. Her clothes and hair were covered in bile and throw-up. Her face and hands were puffy and a little bluish in color. I kept seeing visions of her on the floor and I then I saw visions of a tiled ceiling. Like pictures from a slide show, back and forth, visions of this girl on the floor and the ceiling. "What's going on?", I screamed in the darkness. "What is this I keep seeing?...Who is that?" I begged. With each back and forth vision, the pictures were getting closer and more in detail. I began to see the details of cobwebs on the ceiling and that girl,…as I got a closer look at that girl and realized…THAT WAS ME! "What? She can't be me because I feel fine. I'm in tact and I'm not hurting anywhere. I'm just a little cold and I can't see anything"…I assured myself. It then hit me that there was a separation of my body, spirit and personality. I was having an out-of-body experience. Still shocked by seeing my limp body with no blood circulation, I thought about God and every prayer I've ever prayed.

"Oh my God! ", I cried out loud. Still chilled and in complete darkness, I put my hands over my face in grief and cried again, "Lord help me! Save me Lord! Help me!" Immediately after I cried out, I saw a brilliant light appear above me. It shined as the sun with a white light and not hurtful to the eye. I didn't know what this light was, I just marveled at its brilliance. I've never seen anything glowing bright white before. The light was illuminating from a silhouette image of a man. He has no face or features, just the brilliant light in shape of a man. He came from above and stood right on the left side of me. He looked at me for a minute and tilted his head in compassion. I felt comforted by his presence but I didn't know what he was going to do to me. He was getting closer and closer. The closer he got, the more I could see my surroundings. I was so happy because I recognized that I was still in the bathroom at my job. Nevertheless, I was far more interested in knowing what this image was and what he was doing. Amazingly, he was transparent and he was aligning himself with me. He proceeded to put his foot where my foot was, he placed every toe where mine was. He then sat exactly where I sat and placed his fingers where mine were. He then put his head in the same slopped position that mine was and I opened my eyes. There I was, on the bathroom floor covered in my own mess. I tried to move but it felt like I had piercing pins-and-needles all over my body. My blood started circulating and I began to breathe. Even though I was in pain, it felt great. My body was obeying my mind slowly. I wasn't concerned about anything because I could still see this brilliant glow in me. He knew I was zapped of energy and revitalized himself in me. Imagine an already bright light, getting brighter for a few seconds, and then going back to its original brightness. That's the best way I can explain it.

That boost gave me enough energy to get up and clean up the mess I was in. My throat was dry and I needed water fast. I hadn't said a word yet because I knew that bright image was still in me and I stared in the mirror in awe of it. I washed my face and walked out of the bathroom to call my mother. As I came out of the bathroom, a security guard saw me and was terrified of me. He held on to his radio and kept yelling, "Where did you come from!? Who are you?! Stop right there!" I turned to look at him and he froze with fear. I wonder if he saw what I saw in me. He didn't approach me; rather he got on the radio and was reporting me. I reached for the phone and started dialing my mother. I remember hearing him in the background saying, "I've been here for over 4 hours and I didn't see her go in or out. I need help down here!" I didn't realize it, but I set off motion detector security alarms.

When my mother picked up the phone, she was crying and talking to my boyfriend on the other line. She works for the police department so she called them to help find me. My boyfriend had been driving around downtown Chicago looking for me and was worried sick. The first words I said to her were, "I'm fine. I'm alive. I'm at the job, come and get me. I can't wait to tell you what happened to me!" I explained what I could to the security guards while I waited for my boyfriend to pick me up.

I was rushed to the hospital that night and my doctor said that I must have suffered from a severe case of dehydration and was in a coma. He said usually those are tough to come out of without medical attention. The bluish color meant I lost oxygen for some time. "How you did it with no help is really baffling to me", he said. I told him, while lying in the bed, "I did have help…God saved me. He came and saved me". Some doctors think modern medicine is the only way to go. Little does he know that God is the final physician. He was reluctant to believe that but he admitted that he wouldn't be able to explain my experience.

Wendy Lumpkins

I was released that night and I started telling everyone my amazing story. My sister and mother approached me and asked me, why I thought I was in complete darkness? I really didn't know. They said, "Are you saved?" "Yes", I proclaimed. "Are you delivered?" they asked. "What do you mean? I was dead and now I'm alive, right?" My sister said, "You have to begin aligning your life with God's word and living a Holy life." "But, I'm good, I'm nice, I love God. Isn't that enough?" My sister answered, "You have to go before God and ask Him what He wants you to do. You can't serve two masters. You either love one and hate the other".

I was shaken up by this because I thought that's what my whole experience was about. But I did wonder why everything was so dark, cold and lonely. So I began to seek God. Really search for Him, the way you'd look for a long lost friend or family member. Asking everyone I know. God would reveal things to me and I'd still probe with, "But why?" Slowly God showed me that I was a fornicator; I was vain; I was a liar; I was manipulative and I didn't know God's word for myself. It's tough finding out that you're not what you think you are with God, that what you know isn't enough. It's also hard realizing that your sin is not what makes you who you are. It's not your personality and you shouldn't take it personally when God shows you. I thought that everybody was a fornicator and would tell a lie here or there. But God does not conform to this world; this world must conform to God.

God has blessed me with a second chance when he breathed new life into my dying body. I was born again. Shortly after that, He blessed me with graduating from a four-year college in two years with honors. I broke up with my boyfriend and was celibate for four years until I met and married the husband God handpicked for me. (How He did it, is another amazing story I'll save for another time.) While walking in awe of Him, I was so thankful to God. What seemed like the impossible to most was a wink of an eye from God. Marveling at His greatness, I asked him in the silence of my heart, "Lord, you've done all this for me. All of this for little old me. Christmas is fast approaching and I'm going to ask you….What can I do for you, Lord? Everything I want to know about you and everything I wanted to know about marketing, you've given me. I gave you my life but I feel that's not enough. How can I thank you, Lord?" And in a small still voice, He said, "Market me".

What a concept! Market God. Simple and powerful. Ever since then I have been lead by God to **Deliverance**, which is a free monthly christian publication filled with testimonies. This paper is my testimony. I'm not a journalist, a well-known Christian leader or a person who likes attention. I am the editor of **Deliverance** newspaper and am simply a fellow servant of the Lord's doing what he has called me to do "Market Him".

Email: iwanttotestify@msn.com

Eternal Being

From the beginning, I've been someone else,
Shipwrecked on the jagged rocks of the world,
defending illusions to resist the sprouting of humility
in the hallow garden of my soul.

I pray helplessly but endlessly
for truth to defeat me utterly,

Wendy Lumpkins

that I might stumble upon this
strange, reflective mystery.

The secret voice of God animates my faith,
as I walk undaunted over arid sands of untold anguish
to pass beyond all that can be seen
in search of this invisible source.

I tremble as mirages fade in the one silent vibration.
My heart erupts in spiritual fire,
a portal at the center of being, swallowing me,
as I sink into the unfailing presence of divine love,
anchoring my soul in untainted compassion.

Surrendering to these flames of grace,
I arise reborn like the phoenix,
carried by the wave of life,
stripped of shadows and guarded
by fierce angels with glowing eyes
against the storms of temptation I have known

So that finally, after years of being drenched,
I take root as a seed of truth
at last, piercing the veil to grasp the
first rays of eternal being.

Author Unknown

Reverend Hattie Paulk

Women In Power

Reverend Hattie Paulk

Several years ago, I was faced with a serious back injury. To correct the problem, the doctor performed a new surgical procedure. I later had a reaction to the medication and was transferred to Chanute Air Force Base Hospital. When speaking to the doctor, he informed me that I might have suffered a heart attack. I received nitroglycerine under my tongue and was told that I would need to be medically evacuated or moved to Wright Patterson AFB to consult with a specialist. While at Chanute, a member from my church paid me a visit. She brought me gospel tapes to comfort me. At the time, I was afraid of dying.

As I laid awake; tossing and turning in bed, I began to talk to God. Praying continuously – thanking Him for His many blessings and merciful love. In the midst of my prayer, I saw a vision of a man in a ship. It was raining and lightening and there was a great storm. I heard the man say, "There ain't no danger in the water, because King Jesus is the Captain of this ship". Even though the words filled me with delight, I began to see something evil, dark and scary as I prayed. I was so petrified. I knew that I had to be strong. I cried out, "Satan I rebuke you in the name of Jesus." At that moment; Satan left and Jesus appeared in a long white robe. Immediately, my fears of dying departed.

Before leaving for Wright Patterson AFB, the doctor called my entire family, informing them of his plans to fly me to Ohio.

Hatti Paulk

My daughter Lisa accompanied me on the plane. As we were boarding the plane it began to rain. My youngest daughter, Nicole (Mushie) came out on the runway and kissed me. I could tell that she was worried.

When I arrived in Ohio, the doctor said I had a blockage. He explained that they would need to perform a cauterization which is a procedure performed on the skin or mucosa to effect scarring; often used to remove lesions or control bleeding. Because of possible complications, I was informed that I would need to fill out a form releasing them from any liabilities. But I believed in my heart that there would be no complications and so I completed the form.

On that day, my daughter Lisa spoke to me and told me of a dream she had regarding my mother, who had passed some years ago. She dreamt that my mother called her on the phone to say that she was at her old address at 505 N. Mathew, in Champaign. In her dream, she asked "Why are you calling me Grandmamma? You are dead." I told her, I didn't know why she was dreaming of death.

Later that day they moved a woman into my room that had suffered a heart attack. As I turned to look at her, I saw that her tray was filled with medicine. My heart went out to her because she was crying. I felt she needed a friend, so I prayed for her. I got back into my bed and begin to talk to God. I said "Lord I just want you to heal me, so I don't have to take all that medicine".

My heart began to flip completely over and I could hear him say, "By my stripes you are healed. Look at the clock". I did and it was 5:05 a.m. that Tuesday, morning.

Later that day, the nurses came to prepare me for surgery. They tried to put a heperm lock in my arm and it would not go in. I cried "Oh God help me". A male nurse or technician said jokingly, "He isn't going to help you – I am. In rebuttal I said, "I know you're shame, he has already helped me and will continue to help me". After several attempts another lady came into the room and saw my Bible on the bed. She laid her hand on the Bible and said that she believed that she could get the heperm lock in and that she didn't think it would hurt. Because of her prayer, she was successful. She wheeled me down to the operating room. As we were approaching the elevator I saw a display that read, "When you pray". I asked the attendant to allow me to see the literature. It was the Lord's prayer. I took one and begin to say the Lord's Prayer and kept it near my heart. When I arrived to the operating room, the doctor. said, "What is that in your chest?" He explained that I could not have the material so close to my body. Explaining the importance of being sterile, he put the prayer under my head. He then proceeded to smile and ask me if I wanted to listen to some country and western music. While smiling back at him, I told him no but I would like to hear "Near My God to Thee". He laughed. I continued to say the Lord's Prayer over and over.

The doctor began the procedures on the right side of my heart. He then turned and speaking to his staff stated that I was clear on the right side. Then he checked the left side of my heart. He stated that I was also clear on the left side. Because of the complications, there must be some damage around the muscle of the heart. He told me to lie still that it would burn a little. Looking puzzled, he explained that I was clear there also. There was no doubt in mind, I told him that the Lord had healed me that morning at 5:05 a.m. Remember that I told you

Hatti Paulk

about my daughter Lisa dreaming about death and the old address being 505, that was confirmation of His healing. Since then I have had a number of supernatural experiences that have taught me to always look back with satisfaction and forward with faith.

Lord's Prayer

"After this manner therefore pray ye: Our Father which art in heaven, Hallowed be thy name. Thy kingdom come. Thy will be done in earth, as [it is] in heaven. Give us this day our daily bread. And forgive us our debts, as we forgive our debtors. And lead us not into temptation, but deliver us from evil: For thine is the kingdom, and the power, and the glory, forever. Amen."

Matthew 6: 9-13

Personal Data

Hattie is a native of Champaign, Illinois. Her family was among the first, black settlers in Champaign. They established the first Church of God In Christ. Her mother and father are deceased. Hattie has six brothers and one sister and is the mother of four biological children. She has nine grandchildren and was a foster mother to over 100 foster children.

In recent years, one of the most memorable accomplishments for Hattie happened while she was arranging a visit from Santa at Columbia School on December 20, 1996. That day as Santa arrived on a fire truck, while all festivities were going on, Hattie was summoned over the intercom. She was told that there was an emergency on school grounds, which needed her immediate attention. Upon arriving at the school parking lot, she discovered a parent in distress. The parent was threatening to take her life. Her personal situations had overwhelmed her. She had more than ten children, was homeless, sleeping in cars, and sometimes roomed with one of her sons in a one-bedroom apartment where drugs were being sold. "I can't take this anymore! I give up!" she stated. She was compelled to help this woman. Hattie sought help from several agencies and private citizens. The Housing Authority of Champaign County provided her with a four-bedroom unit and all of her problems appeared to be solved; unfortunately, they were not. The parent also needed to get her utilities on, but still had previous bills totaling $1,200.00. Hattie continued to contact local agencies and help poured in from everywhere. On Christmas morning the mother and her family were in their new home. She felt good about her faith in people still being humanitarians, and their innate sense of community.

Her second accomplishment was earning a Bachelor of Arts/Sociology from Eastern Illinois University. She still remembers being told by her high school counselor that she wasn't "college material". She recalls working as a domestic and saying to herself that she had the ability to do and be much more, and today she is. She also earned an associate degree from Parkland College, a Bachelor degree from Eastern Illinois University and attended Charles Harrison Mason School of Theology. She has also earned credit through the United States Air Force in Kaiseslaughter, Germany. Currently, Hattie is pursuing a graduate degree in Guidance and Counseling. In 1989, she was one of eight people in the

Hatti Paulk

United States to be named an "Outstanding Adult Learner" and was honored in Washington, D.C.

In spite of the challenges of work, marriage, four natural children and over 100 foster children, she continues to strive to be a lifelong learner. Through hard work, determination, and much prayer, she has been able to fulfill her dreams and realize that she is "college material" after all.

Disappointments

One of her greatest disappointments was when she had to transport a parent from the county courthouse. After leaving the courthouse the parent requested a ride to a local grocery store to buy some candles. This parent had her utilities shut off and Hattie had volunteered to let her children stay at her home until they found a way to get her utilities turned back on. She needed the candles to see at night. The parent asked Hattie for some money to purchase the candles. Hattie gave her the money and waited in the car for her return. After an unusually long period of time, the parent came running out of the store being pursued by a man, who then escorted her back into the store. She was stealing and the grocery store management had called the police, so they waited for them to come. When the police arrived, she began to lie about the incident and gave them false personal information. Hattie explained to the police who she was and the circumstances leading up to the incident. The police allowed her to take the parent home.

Being employed by the social district, she is always burdened by problems that she feel has not been addressed. Hatti says, "the lack of communication between children and their parents who have been incarcerated is a serious concern for me." She wants to help bridge this gap between the parent and the child and help to create a more stable learning environment.

Professional Experience

Hattie Paulk is the director of the Champaign Unit 4 School District Family Information Center. There she has spearheaded the countywide Community-Kid-Link program, which includes the Warm-A-Kid Drive where the goal is to insure that children are provided with warm clothing. She works as a parent coordinator for Columbia Elementary School and teacher assistant for Roberson Elementary School. She is an ordained minister, who has addressed congregation in California, Louisiana, Indiana, Illinois, Ughele, Nigeria, Africa and numerous other places. She formally served as assistance pastor at Church of Living God in Chicago, Illinois. She received an Illinois State Board of Education "Those Who Excel Award" for educational personnel and a Unit 4 Board of Education Award of Recognition. She speaks annually at the Black History program at the Danville Correctional Institution and has received the Mother Consella York Award. Hattie has also been the Keynote speaker for the National Adult and Continuing Education Conference. In addition, she has had the privilege of addressing Wori Girls School in Ugahle, Nigeria Africa. She has been the guest speaker for many public information and news program on WCIA, WILL-TVs.

Hedy Ratner

Women In Power

Hedy Ratner

*N*ever doubt that a small group of individuals can change the world. Indeed, it is the only thing that ever has. Hedy Ratner is one of those rare individuals that has dedicated herself to starting and leading many of those small groups of individuals and she has indeed changed our world for the better.

1986 was the year of Chernobyl, the Challenger tragedy, the election of Corazon Aquino, and, in Illinois, the birth of a small non-profit, the Women's Business Development Center. It was started by two women with a great idea: to create a place to help women with their dreams of entrepreneurship, a place where women would create new jobs, new lives, new selves by starting and running businesses.

Moved by their frustration with basic social service programs and inspired by their own experiences in the business sector, Hedy Ratner and her business partner Carol Dougal felt that economic power and strength through entrepreneurship was the path out of poverty, dead-end jobs, and the glass ceiling faced by so many women. This small idea was truly a vision at the time, only 15% of all business were owned by women. Women's entrepreneurship was an economic and social tool not recognized as valid by any of the major public policy and programmatic systems in our country: the federal government, the state, the city had none, and none of the foundations had programs to supporting women's entrepreneurship. Support for this endeavor was non-existent.

And yet Hedy and Carol were able to open the WBDC through sheer determination and a strong belief in the capacity of women to start their own businesses and do well. They are working also towards a persuasive vision of a world wherein women entrepreneurs were leaders, power brokers, and taking businesses and families in new and healthy directions.

Hedy knocked on the doors of prospective supporters convincing a few that the Women's Business Development Center was a powerful idea that needed to come to fruition- and the journey to providing support to women business owners began.

Some would consider Hedy a risk-taker. She started the WBDC, its programs, and its advocacy initiatives with just a small idea, without much financial support or even public goodwill. But I think Hedy would disagree. She would say "Of course the WBDC worked and still works. It makes sense, we needed to do it then and we still need to do it!" She is able to see what should be, what is possible, and she makes it real.

Hedy's ability to see the possibilities permeates her life. She sees those possibilities in dozens of young women. She often hires, mentors or coaches women who show upon her doorstep without any business experience, without any expertise in the non-profit sector, appearing only with a certain eagerness and a desire to "help people." Hedy's leap of faith inspires and moves them. Sitting at the feet of the master they earned advanced degree in Feminism and

Organizing. They launch their own small business, complete their bachelors and or masters, and become successful, driven business women. In fact, many of the people working at the WBDC are business owners hired as consultants, and several employees have left the organization with the intent of starting their own businesses, always with Hedy's support. She helps others understand the critical nature of this work, empowering through example, information, and energy.

20 years after its founding, the WBDC is now the most comprehensive business service center for women in the United States. Each year the WBDC serves over 12,000 women in the Chicagoland area-helping them get their businesses started or strengthened. The local and national policies that Hedy has helped create have made home businesses legal in the city of Chicago; secured ongoing business opportunities for women in the public sector; fought institutionalized sexism and racism; created federal streams of funding for women entrepreneurs; and secured new sources of financing for microbusinesses owned by women.

The organization has secured funding from the private sector, respected foundations, and many governmental entities. Hedy and her team has created and nurtured an organization that inspires and will be sustained for another two decades and beyond. They have assisted women in fourteen other states launch their own women's business centers and have also helped women in other countries start organizations focusing on women's entrepreneurship.

It is Hedy's fire that drives the Women's Business Development Center. Once you have met her, you see her everywhere. She is giving speeches, she is giving testimony to legislative committees, she is in the newspaper talking about women in business, she is at the governor's office helping to find support for women's programs, she is on the radio discussing access to financing for microenterprises, she is at the White House advocating for sustained funding for women's. She has done more than anyone in the country to change policy regarding women's business ownership. She is able to help policymakers see the importance of and then implement women's business ownership programs and policies.

Hedy's energy and attitude keeps her developing good ideas and getting them implemented. Talking about new ways of better serving the women who count on the Women's Business Development Center to launch or develop their businesses, Hedy will say, "Let's call her and get this going." It does not matter who she needs to contact; it could be a Foundation staff person or the Mayor, she will get that person on the phone to get the ball rolling.

Hedy also serves as an information hub. She can recall facts and statistics about women's business ownership in an instant, she can say who's working on what regarding women's economic development in any given part of the country, and she can speculate with an amazing degree of accuracy the shape of things to come on policy and trends for women business owners. Her phone rings off the hook, her e-mail inbox is filled with people needing guidance, information, facts, figures, statements, and Hedy's wisdom.

Driven by her belief in the equality of women and fueled by her visionary character, Hedy has influenced and changed the lives of so many people through the WBDC and through the creation of better public policy: from the single mother leaving a dead-end career to start her own business to the banker whose views on women business owners are changed as he makes lending decisions; from the recent graduate student looking for a job that will make an impact to the staff person leaving to start her own business. Countless women's lives have been changed because of Hedy's vision and her work to create a powerful economic revolution wherein women enact their dream of prospering through business ownership.

Appointments

An advocate and activist for women's issues for the past 30 years, Hedy Ratner was appointed by the President to the National Women's Business Council; was appointed by former Illinois Governor Edgar and current Governor Ryan to the Illinois Women's Business Ownership Council that she helped to advocate for and create; and was appointed by both Governors to serve on the Governor's Commission on the Status of Women in Illinois. Chicago Mayor Richard Daley appointed Hedy as Co-Chairperson of the Women's Health Task Force. She is also a board member of the Chicagoland Chamber of Commerce and the Chicago Convention and Tourism Bureau; a founding member of the Coalition for Equal Opportunity, The Alliance of Minority and Female Contractors Association, and the National Council of Women's Organizations. She has been honored by U.S.S.B.A., National Association of Women Business Owners, YWCA, and Federation of Women Contractors.

Nilsa Reyna

Nilsa Reyna

"You came from nothing."

The words echoed in my brain as I sat and stared at what my husband had just said to me. At that moment I wondered if the people sitting next to us overheard what he had just said. It was kind of loud and certainly anyone passing by who heard him might have assumed that he was some kind of monster who abuses his wife.

What they didn't know is we were in the middle of a heated discussion regarding my career. You see, I have two careers. I am an Executive Assistant by day. Yes, the job that pays the bills. By night or rather anytime I can squeeze it in, I am an actress. This has been my lifestyle ever since I moved to Chicago to pursue an acting career.

It's funny how people back home already see me as a big success and I can't understand why. Personally, I believe that I have along way to travel to be successful. But then I am very critical of myself and often create unattainable standards.

Success takes on a different meaning for each individual. Sometimes I believe I am not a successful actress because I still hold a day job. I mean, sure, my acting resume is beginning to look promising and I have been paid for various theatre and on camera projects, but I am not yet a part of any acting unions (i.e., Screen Actors Guild, American Federation of Theatrical Radio Artists and Equity Actors Association).

For this reason, many do not see me as a professional actress or a successful one. Personally I believe getting paid to act entitles one to be labeled as a professional, although I still do believe I have so much still to learn. What is soothing to my soul is I have my whole life ahead of me to move up in levels of success.

Okay, now back to my husband's comment, "You came from nothing." Yes, that is true and the comment was not meant to belittle me in anyway. You see, I am a fourth generation Texan born Latina with roots in Mexico and Spain. I was born in McAllen, Texas and grew up in San Juan, Texas. Back home everyone is so in tune with the Mexican culture that many of the stereotypes portrayed in the media, television, and movies really are true. I always say stereotypes hold some truth to them or else they wouldn't exist. One stereotype held truth for my family. Our meals consist of rice, beans and tortillas. Almost all of my family can spit out Spanish and English at the drop of a hat. We come from a strong Catholic background and many still believe that women should not work.

While I love my family, there are things about them I've learned to accept. These were things I was ashamed of as a child growing up. For example, my family was poor and my mother didn't work. While I was happy to have my mom around, her unemployment caused a financial strain on the family. She did a wonderful job raising my brother, sisters and I, the fact that she didn't work caused financial strain for a family of six. My father on the other hand, supported us by being a Gunsmith. Although, he was a very popular man back home because Texans love guns and hunting, his job many times hovered on merely being a hobby. Thankfully, other family members were generous and often times helped with additional necessities.   Sometimes we even had the latest trend in jeans or the must have toy of the Christmas season.

The comment, "You came from nothing," refers to a lack of financial means. I beat the odds and surpassed generations in my family in terms of success, pursuing my dreams and financial well being. To this day, my family often sit around talking about what they really wanted to be or if they could only be something else in life. Financially, my acting career borders on being a hobby, while my second career allows me to keep my dream alive and live very comfortably. The fact that I don't do mindless work all of the day also helps keep me going.

So, as you can imagine, my family was not supportive when news broke that I wanted to go to college out of state and major in theatre. Sure, they had seen me in high school plays and always commented on my talent or how pretty I looked on stage, but they simply thought it was a good way for me to stay out of trouble. Only one of my cousins had gone away to school to study architecture, a few hours away from home.

After repeatedly answering questions about how I planned to raise a family as an actress, holding a position that no husband would approve, I finally was able to convince them I was going to be fine because I had received many scholarships and had thoroughly researched each school's safety and academic record. Finally, their blessing was granted and everyone agreed they wouldn't prevent me from pursuing my dreams. I think they knew deep down inside that I would have pursued college anyway, at least it was college and not New York where most aspiring actors/actresses migrate.

So, off I went to Webster University in Saint Louis, Missouri where I enrolled in the Conservatory Theatre of Fine Arts and became one of the token Latinas. I didn't mind at all, not at first; however, later on I began to doubt I had talent and started to wonder if I was there because the school needed to make their quota. Nevertheless, I worked hard trying to rid myself of bad acting habits.

At the end of two years, the theatre faculty held evaluations and made decisions to either cut or keep people. It was no surprise I was let go as I always seemed to be on the cusp of advancing to the next level in my process, but could never seem to make that leap. The faculty felt little progress was made and I often lacked an emotional connection when acting. The progress I made at the end was "too little too late." This can be a painful time for many hopefuls, but surprisingly I had the most confidence in my acting in a long time. After a talk with the Dean of the College of Fine Arts, I was persuaded to transition to a college with a strong acting program in Chicago. He believed Chicago to be a great town for a new start.

I auditioned for Roosevelt University's theatre program and got accepted into the acting program on the spot. In the midst of it all, I met my future husband at Webster, a Business Administration major. Sadly, I would be leaving him behind, but our deep connection meant we could survive a long distance relationship. I also knew we would get married someday.

The transition to Chicago proved difficult. I was unhappy with the school and appalled that many theatre majors skipped acting classes on a regular basis. This was supposedly something they loved. I also discovered I was in culture shock and had been sheltered growing up. To make matters worse, I missed my future husband terribly.

Then I started thinking, how can I become a good actress if I haven't been exposed to much of the world? I realized I couldn't be. In addition, I realized I often suppressed my feelings, a defense mechanism my whole family employs and it was hindering my character portrayals. Theatre couldn't be my only focus. A program where I could eat, breathe and sleep theatre at a young age was not the right program for me. I was already enrolled at a school with a program that fit my learning style, but it was in transition.

After much thought, I gathered my stuff and ran away with my future husband back to St. Louis in the middle of the night. He was about to start his last semester and I wanted to be with him. I knew I didn't want to go back home and so I decided to transfer to another Saint Louis school.

My parents didn't know what to say, especially when I told them we had moved in together. They must have thought I was another failed actress, another statistic, another Latina who tried to make something of herself, but ended up with a mess of problems.

This is where my future husband comes in. You see, he inadvertently helped me to grow as an actress. He gave me a deeper exposure to other worlds such as sports, the stock market and politics. He reminded me that being alive was not about living a life that completely revolves around theatre.

A year and a half later, I received a B.A. from Saint Louis University in Theatre Performance. I had not only proved to myself but to my entire family that this was an attainable goal. They were also now fully supportive of my decision to move back to Chicago and pursue an acting career. They didn't even mind I would still be living with my boyfriend and after a couple of years of prayer, my mom got her wish and we were married.

As you can imagine, things are more challenging now then ever before. Even though I am blessed to have agent representation and I have had some success as an actress, it is still difficult to find the time to practice new audition pieces, market myself, operate my acting career as a business, go see theatre and movies as much as possible, take classes to further my training, work my day job, spend time with my husband, visit my family in Texas, and the list goes on.

What keeps me going is not only my love of acting and knowing that being onstage or in a film portraying a certain character may open someone's eyes to something new and actually improve their lives, but also that I can be a role model and change stereotypes of Latinas.

Latinas and Latinos don't see ourselves accurately portrayed in the entertainment industry. I hope to inspire other Latinas to become actresses and prove that a career in the arts is possible. It is not easy, but it can be done and I am proof of it.

I am now Teatro Luna's Reading Series Director (Chicago's all Latina theatre company in which I am an ensemble member). The Reading Series' aim is to give new and established playwrights a chance to be heard. In addition, Teatro Luna has reawakened my writing skills and few of the pieces have been produced.

Being part of this ensemble makes it more difficult to balance our lives. We have our own theatre space and with that comes the struggle to make rent and pay utilities. We often wear many hats in our company and I will be the first to admit I am not always fond of it. Nevertheless, there is a strong need for us to exist as evidenced by selling out shows on a consistent basis, being invited to perform around the country and seeing new fans emerge each time we produce a show.

Next time someone tells me I lack a connection to my character; I will smile, accept it as constructive criticism, take notes, make an adjustment, and move on.

Success

To laugh often and much;
To win the respect of intelligent people
And the affection of children;
To earn the appreciation of honest critics
And endure the betrayal of false friends;
to appreciate beauty,
to find the best in others;
to leave the world a bit better
whether by a healthy child,
a garden patch,
or a redeemed social condition;
to know even one life
has breathed easier because you have lived,
This is to have succeeded.

Ralph Waldo Emerson

*Alice Faye
Katrina
Rodriquez*

Women In Power

Alice Faye Katrina Rodriguez

On a daily basis, the people you meet are attempting to change their lives in some way. Generally speaking, people crave hope, financial freedom, good health, unconditional love, a well-developed soul, a definite major purpose, and spiritual fulfillment.

Because I was born as the tenth child into a healthy spiritual environment, I recognized at an early age, that I was gifted by God and able to do all things through His power. **I discovered the power of the spoken word, faith based work, and the unadulterated love of Jesus Christ.** My parents had borne nine boys before me, and as the last child, and the only girl, it became necessary for me to develop strong coping and vocal skills. I had to learn to speak emphatically, and with intense persuasion at the age of three or four years old, just to get my brothers to take me with them when they were going out to play. I had to learn to stand up for myself physically, without fear, because my brothers would not tolerate a wimp, and it did not matter to them that I was a girl. My parents were in a non-traditional, outreach ministry. As a child in their home, **I discovered that blessed people were usually courageous people. They were problem solvers in the lives of other people. Blessed people were sometimes controversial because they refused to be average, so that people around them would feel comfortable.**

Our little home was always crowded with someone, other than the family, who had problems to be solved. Pregnant teenage girls would stop by, spending countless hours with my mother. They needed desperately to be encouraged, and to have someone speak wisdom into their lives. A wife whose husband was in jail after a weekend drunken spree, would come by and ask my Father if he would go down to the jail with her to sign papers, so that her husband could come home and not lose his job. There were times when there were as many as fourteen people sleeping in that tiny little two bedroom home, and the floor was regularly strewn with pillows and bed pallets. Cousins, friends, acquaintances, and foes, would come to the door from 5:00 a.m. until well after midnight to talk with my parents, commonly known in the community as Uncle Jasper, and Aunt Ruby. In the early days, we had no money, but my parents, by their Godly influence and good reputation in the community, were great problem solvers in the lives of other people. I would watch my Mother cook hoe cake corn bread on the stove, and with some neighbor's baby on one hip, she would stir the flour, dispense sage advise, and feed what seemed to be a multitude off of one cabbage. At the age of three, I would stare at the knees of the adults, and stand boldly in the middle of the conversational fray, giving my little three year old opinion, whether anybody listened to me or not. My parents, keenly in tuned to the gifts of their children, began to call me their little lawyer. The confidence shown in me by my parents, and their strong faith in God, instilled in me a belief and passionate longing to defend the underdog.

Therefore, I tried cases before my dolls in that tiny block home in a small rural town in South Georgia. I tried cases under the pecan and pear trees, in the cotton fields, the peanut fields, on the playground and Sunday school. Wherever I could find someone who would listen to me, or who would be still for five minutes, I became an advocate of an idea, a cause, a mission, and a purpose. I defended my brothers when one of them failed to perform a chore that my Father had ordered.

In fourth grade, I was known as the boss by all of my little friends, because inevitably, I could persuade them to follow my lead. I would ask the teachers in elementary school, "why", "why", "why"?!? My Father and Mother often said that they marveled at my courage, because I would question them, and even question why we lived in such a tiny house if God was so great!

I will never forget when I discovered **why loving Jesus alone would not make you wealthy, or healthy, or complete.** When I discovered that Jesus was never going to come down and buy me a bicycle, that he was not going to make Mama let me go to a party, that he was not going to give me the money for my college tuition, I truly became aware of my role in life and in the lives of other people. Though I believed in God and His Son, I recognized that **it was my job to renew and train the beautiful mind, which he had given me, and to intelligently equip myself to obtain the things I wanted in life.** It was at this time that proper thought process plus proper work ethic helped me to begin to be an even greater problem solver for myself and for other people.

I grew mightily in the process, because initially, if I could not win with words, I would not hesitate to get into a fistfight. Since my sibling role models were boys, my oldest brother made me learn karate, and self-defense. I played sports and loved basketball with a passion. I would play basketball outside in the cold, and my hands would be frozen. I would play ball in the sweltering South Georgia heat until I looked as if I had been washed down with a fire hydrant. In any game I was playing I would talk much smack, I had learned to combine words with actions and to solve problems. I would

Alice Faye Katrina Rodriguez

look onto the basketball court for the problems, and tell the coach where our defense needed fixing, or where they had a weakness in their defense. A big mouth will get some attention; but a big mouth, backed up with sound thought process, down-home courage, and proper work habits resulted in a young black female lawyer.

When the recruiters came from the University of Georgia (UGA) and sat me down in a classroom, I was the only student out of a senior class of about 150 students that they came to talk to. My coach, Jessie McCloud, had called them. He had run my guts out on the basketball court, and helped me tame my tongue so that I only ended up in one fight in my senior year of high school. He demanded that I have good grades. That man, along with my parents and brothers, taught me mental and physical discipline, as well as, problem solving skills. If I came into the gym with a "C" on my report card, my coach made the whole team run blood and guts and suicide drills. Since my parents were still not wealthy people, and we were still living in that two bedroom block home, I had already enrolled in Mercer University in Macon, Georgia at the time UGA came to recruit. I had been accepted into a two-year paralegal program at Mercer and figured that after I graduated and worked for a few years, I could put myself through law school. I could not envision at that time getting a four-year college degree because there wasn't any money. When I was told that I qualified for a full scholarship at a four-year college, I walked around in a dream world for the rest of the school day. I blabbed to all of my friends, white and black, Jew and Gentile . . . whoever would listen. Some were happy for me, and some were envious. When the bell ranged, I raced home to convince my Father that it was alright for us to lose the tuition money we had already paid to Mercer University because I was going to the University of Georgia! With much

Women In Power

trepidation, I launched into one of the greatest closing arguments of my young life, and when I was through, my Daddy jumped up and started dancing!

He said, "Forget the tuition we already paid, this is what I wanted for you all along!" Eight years later I was graduating law school.

After many struggles in a university system, which Charlayne Hunter Gault, a powerful woman in her own right, helped to integrate, I had a law degree. I had traveled all over the nation representing the University in Moot Court competitions, and in my second year of law school, Carla Young, now a District Attorney and I, placed second in the Nation as great orators. I had finally been recognized for what I did best, and I subsequently received a license, and would be paid to do it! I have (along with God's grace and the help of wonderful people) been able to create a lifestyle I had never dreamed possible, by solving other people's problems with the power of words and smart work.

My childhood journey, with the right foundation, resulted years later in my being the first black woman, born and raised in the State of George, to ever serve in 200 years on the Georgia Court of Appeals. Justice Robert Benham, now a Georgia Supreme Court Justice gave me my first chance at honing my skills in the legal arena. He believed in me and reaffirmed my upbringing.

At the time that Judge Benham hired me as a Law Clerk, he was the first black man ever, in 200 years to serve as a Judge on the Georgia Court of Appeals. Other than my father and my high school basketball coach, Judge Benham was the first true male mentor I had. His words to me were like the words of God. He had a beautiful family in Cartersville, Georgia,

Alice Faye Katrina Rodriguez

very down to earth, principled, and he loved God. Judge Benham was not ashamed of his humble past, and he inspired me. I left his employ with a freshly trained mind and professionally tamed tongue backed up by a proper work ethic, proper thought process, and an even greater faith in God. I competed with young law students all over the nation and was selected and blessed to serve as a Legal Intern on the Hill in Washington D.C. for Senator Sam Nunn and I then furthered my legal studies in the Governor's Intern Program on the Hill in Atlanta, Georgia.

Today, I along with my husband, Anthony P. Rodriguez, own and operate three very successful businesses as well as a law practice. It is all because I learned to help other people solve their problems while learning to conquer my own mind, discipline my habits, and harness the power of the spoken word. I cannot in good conscious have people read about me and not know that I was simply then, and am now, a willing vessel, eager to learn, willing to fight, and blessed because the people whom I have mentioned helped me. Even today, I am continually blessed by great people. Therefore, my goal is to continue to help as many people as possible before I call it quits here on earth, and move on to eternal life.

In the interim, I aspire to continue to develop friendship with people like Sheila Downer, the author of this publication. I expect to utilize every gift I have, before God calls me home. And since I have never written a book, its time that I sat at the feet of people like Sheila Downer and Robyn Williams, author of *Preconceived Notions* and *A Twist of Fate*, as we still have much work to do, and many more problems in our world to solve.

Fear

"Our biggest fear is not that we are inadequate. Our deepest fear is that we are powerful beyond measure. It is our light, not our darkness, that most frightens us. We ask ourselves, who am I to be brilliant, gorgeous, talented and fabulous? Actually, who are you not to be? You are a child of God. Your playing small doesn't serve the world. There's nothing enlightened about shrinking so that other people won't feel insecure around you. We were born to make manifest the glory of God that is within us. It's not just in some of us; it's in everyone. And as we let our own light shine, we unconsciously give other people permission to do the same. As we are liberated from our own fear, our presence automatically liberates others. And excellence becomes the standard of all our lives."

Marianne Williamson
(quoted in the Nelson Mandela
Inaugural Speech, 1994)

Susan Rosen

Women In Power

Susan Rosen

Being a nurse means many different things to many different people. Personally, I believe that you are lead by your own experiences. There is one experience I believe that lent a hand in my decision to become a Registered Nurse.

In 1972, on my way to grammar school, I fell and broke my leg. My mother rushed me to the hospital and I spent all day and a better part of the night there. I was in a lot of pain and I did not know what to expect. I had never been in a hospital before. I was being moved from one examination room to another and the pain was excruciating. I held onto my mother and I cried. Even though I was young, I was not afraid. I discovered that I was fascinated by the dynamics of the hospital. Everything seemed to be much bigger then me. The building was tall and the people were unfamiliar and still I was intrigued. After a while, someone called my name and a very kind person all dressed in white came out to meet me. She was friendly and warm. She talked to me and explained what had happened with my leg. She made me feel very comfortable and I almost forgot about the pain. She explained that my leg would be put in a cast and that my friends could sign it. She even offered to be the first one to sign my cast. She took so much time out with me that I almost forgot that my leg was broke. She explained that it would be awhile before my leg would heal but most importantly she taught me how to walk on crutches.

Susan Rosen

I truly believe that was the moment that changed my life forever.

In 1979, I went into high school fueled with admiration, persistence and determination of becoming a nurse. I even surrounded myself with people who wanted the same career. I took the exam for the LPN program along with three other friends. To my surprise, we were the only ones who passed out of a room filled with students. Although, I worked very hard in high school, I somehow lost focus and did not complete the entire program. I just convinced myself that it was due to adolescent. But I knew better. I knew that if I wanted to be a nurse I would have to apply and be more committed to myself.

In 1983, I graduated from high school and began college. I completed the necessary pre-requisites and finally entered the Nursing program. I did very well my first quarter, but by my second quarter, I became distracted. I met someone and I fell deeply in love. Unfortunately, the romance ended abruptly and I was very sad and hurt, which led to my inability eat, sleep or concentrate. In the process I lost over 30 pounds. I was at a crossroad and did not know where to turn.

My family strongly suggested that I take up another career. But there was no other alternative for me. I love nursing and medicine was my life and the thought of not being able to bring comfort to others while helping them to heal was just not an option.

By the time I figured it all out, I had failed my 2nd quarter. I needed to make wise decisions and so I sat out the next semester to regroup. That time away allowed me the opportunity to regroup, refocus and reflect on what truly mattered in life – Nursing.

I knew that nursing to me was like breathing; it was something I had to do in order to survive. Eventually, I returned to school in my persistence to complete school, I learned a great deal about myself and about nursing. In general, I learned that I not only had to care for others but I had to make a moral commitment to care for myself. I had to determine what was good for me and what wasn't. I had to understand that anything worth having is worth working for.

After graduating in 1989, I acquired a position in labor and delivery. Being able to work with children has been a dream come true and a life-long passion met. I truly love the work I do and when I held the first child I helped to deliver, my heart stopped. I never thought that I could see something more amazing then a child taking its first breath and after many births later, it still astonishes me.

A child is a special gift from God and I've learned to appreciate each child for its different personality. But after many deliveries I see how each child is different and have their own personality. I find working with children requires patience and a good heart, as well as the ability to stay calm and to be conscientious.

But even though there is much beauty in nursing, one incident almost caused me to rethink my decision. One day, the head nurse of our department and I were entangled in a feud. The original cause of our argument is unimportant, but to say the least for the sake of our work, I knew that I had to find a way to work with her cordially and professionally. People were counting on us. It was very stressful this day. Nothing seemed to go right. She seemed to overlook all of my accomplishments for that day, while complimenting another new nurse's skill. She complained about anything and everything that I had done. That would have not bothered me so if her body language and words were not so offensive.

That evening, I left the hospital stressed and feeling as though I had accomplished very little, thinking to myself that nursing was not all it was cracked up to be.

When I made it home, my mother had received in the mail my board results. I collapsed in my living room chair, loudly venting about my difficult day on the job.

My mother replied, "Just forget about that and open the envelope". Because I was still complaining, she opened the envelope and stated that I had passed. I grabbed the envelope and stated, "it does not say pass". Because I was so overwhelmed with what had taken place earlier, I overlooked the "pass" comment. Finally, the words "pass" came into view. That one-second put everything into perspective. Everything that I wanted at that moment in life was finally brought to fruition and no human being could take that away from me. I had worked too hard and too long to achieve this success.

To say the least, I went back to work with a whole different view on dealing with difficult people. I had to fine a way to effectively turn a negative situation into a positive one by changing my behavior. I believe this would hopefully impact a better result.

The head nurse and I eventually, were able to put the past behind us and move forward. I discovered for myself that when things get tough, as it sometimes will, more patience is needed. It is not the job but another human being that I am dealing with.

I have also discovered this truth for myself that even though parts of my job are not pleasant, especially when a child dies, I still can't complain. My belief is that after an innocent infant or child dies; an angel is waiting to be born.

In my role as a nurse, I have vowed to protect as many children as I can. I believe that many deaths could be prevented through proper training and education. Therefore, I now conduct workshops and seminars, educating the public on reducing the risk of Sudden Infant Death Syndrome (SIDs). I've also appeared in **Jet Magazine** in the early 90's in reference to my work with newborns.

As a result, I know that nursing is one of the most positive decisions I've ever made in life.

Persistence

"Nothing in the world can take place of persistence. Talent will not; nothing is more common than unsuccessful men with talent. Genius will not; unrewarded genius is almost a proverb. Education will not; the world is full of educated derelicts. Persistence and determination alone are omnipotent."

Calvin Coolidge

Mary Smith

Women In Power

Mary Smith

> "don't forget that you shape the future
> by whom you teach today"

*I*f someone had told me that I would have 4 children, a home in Illinois, and run my own businesses, I would have told them "YEAH RIGHT"!

I was born and raised in Brookhaven, MS. October 3, 1963. Well at least I thought the 3rd. For 17 years, I have celebrated my birthday on October 3, but when I got ready to graduate from high school, I had to present a copy of my birth certificate, which read born on October 4. Wow – what a surprise! This was the first of many surprises to come.

When I was 16th years old, my mother relocated to Chicago, Illinois. She took with her my younger brother, leaving behind me and my other siblings to live with our dad. At that time there was not enough money for all to go but upon graduation from high school; it was custom for us to take our suitcase to the ceremony and when it was over, we would go directly to the train station. My Mom would provide us with a one-way ticket to Chicago to live with a relative. Because we did not have a lot of money growing up, we were taught the value of the almighty dollar. Most of our things were hand-me-downs and when we received a new item, we had to take extra care of it in order to pass it down to someone else. On Christmas the youngest babies were the only ones to receive gifts. I can remember once, my older brother did not receive

Mary Smith

anything for Christmas and he cried. He ran away from home for only 2 hours and I can remember the hurt expression on his face. I knew then that I would never want my child(ren) to suffer such pain and in order to prevent them from enduring such a hardship, I would need to continue my education. College is important. To me, it meant the difference between poverty or a better life.

After graduation from high school, I attended Copiah Lincoln Community College and received my associate degree. I knew that in order to further my career, I would have to attend a 4-year college. In my search for school, I decided to go to college out of state. I was engaged at the time so this was a very hard decision for me. But if you want to be successful in life, you have to make sacrifices. I believe that college can expand your knowledge, increase your potential and assist you in earning more money.

I discussed my decision with my fiancé and he did not share in my enthusiasm to move to Chicago. After careful consideration, I wrote him a 4-page letter and explained my decision. I encouraged him to change his mind and join me but he did not budge. Not being able to face him, I had my brother to hand deliver the letter to him and the beginning of my letter stated, " When you receive this letter I will be in Memphis, on my way to Chicago". He was very hurt by my decision but wished me the very best. He never changed his mind to follow me and I never looked back.

Chicago was a big city and seemed intimidating for a young naive country girl. I thought I had learned a lot from the people around me but I was shocked at the differences in the way things were. Young people made their own decisions, they talked back to their parents, and they were having babies at a very young age. This was all new to me. Soon I began to expect things to be different from the way I was raised. I still held on to my values yet I didn't expect others to share my beliefs. I was anxious when I got to Chicago. I contacted a local college and found that they were very expensive and I could not afford to attend right away. I wanted to keep my independence, to be my own person, make my own decisions and be responsible for my own outcome. Therefore, I decided to look for work.

At this time, my mother lived in Maywood and would give me money to buy a Sunday, Chicago Tribune. I would contact potential job leads, send out tons of resumes weekly and still no responses. I then decided to look for work outside of my field. The phone began to ring but there only seemed to be an interest for lower paying jobs. I became a little discouraged with the whole job search process, but finally after 8 months, I was offered a job. When the manager from Walgreens called I was so excited, that I did not hesitate before taking the job. It was part-time and paying minimum wage. I was extremely happy because this was my first job ever. With this part-time job, I was able to get my first apartment. Later on, I got pregnant with my first daughter, Terinosha. She was really the driving force behind my decision to seek full time employment. Now I was on my way. I was working full time and my mother moved in with me to take care of my baby. This gave me the opportunity to go back to school and enhance my office skills. Things seemed to be looking a lot better. I left my job at Walgreens and took a position with my oldest sister's company, which paid more and had much more potential for growth. This job was in the suburbs so I needed a car to get there. I worked for a month and purchased my first car. A four door Chevy Spectrum, brown with pin stripes. One year later, I married Teri's father. He lived on the west side of Chicago and not in the best of neighborhoods. I was a little apprehensive about living there. He had resided on the west side of Chicago for so long and didn't want to move outside of his comfort zone. One day while in the hospital having Tyneisha, our second child, one of the neighbors broke into our home and took our belongings. I felt like someone had invaded our privacy. I was convinced that it was now time to move.

I searched and found an apartment in Maywood. The rent was much higher and I knew that we would need to travel a distance into the city for our childcare. But sacrifices would have to be made for the safety of our kids. I packed up our things and said to my husband that we were moving. We moved but bills were mounting and we were falling behind. My brother-n-law found a higher paying full-time job with benefits for my husband and I thought things were looking up again, but each year we would move. I started feeling the need for stability for my children and I desired a home to raise them. This would be our next project. As our lives progressed, I began to notice that my husband and I were totally opposite in regards to desire and personal growth. He never required more and was always happy with status quo. But I wanted and needed more.

I wanted a house so desperately, I started working two part-time jobs along with my full-time job. I worked nights and weekends. I was spending more time at work and less with my family. I tried to justify it by saying "it was for a good cause" and on March 31, we signed a contract for our first house. I remember my sister saying to me before I took my night job, "don't take a second job because your husband will do less with you taking care of more." I, of course did not listen, and that's exactly what happened. Things were not working out. We argued over trivial matters. We found ourselves distant and to add insult to injury, my husband cheated on me, which led to our divorce.

What was I going to do? We had just signed a contract on a house. I had to contact the mortgage broker and the realtor and try to renegotiate the terms and see if I could get the house in my name only, but unfortunately I could not. I called my Dad and asked him to co-sign. All my life I felt as though my Mom has made all of the sacrifices, it was now his turn. I was in tears yet still very strong about what I wanted to do. My Dad hesitantly agreed and the following September, my children and I moved into our house. By December of that year, I was legally divorced. My divorce papers were the first ornament on our Christmas tree in our new home.

With lack of a male figure and a second provider, my priorities had to change. I had to quit both of my part-time jobs to be at home with my children. I could not take them to my mothers anymore because I lived farther west. I didn't have their father around to help with backup care when I needed it. Childcare became almost impossible for me. My children were in school full time now and there were limited programs in my area for afterschoolers. In April 1996 I began my research on how to create a home based childcare. There seem to be a great need because there were very few in the area. I took classes while still working and obtained all of the documents needed to start my business.

In the meantime, my children were still attending the afterschool program. One day I inquired with the provider about how my child's day was and she indicated that she did not have the time to tell me everyday how my child day was. I was thrown by her comment. It made me a little apprehensive about my child's care. How could you not be concerned about a child's welfare? That very same week, I complained that my child had witnessed some behavioral issues of another child. The person in charge informed me, I was attempting to cause problems. I explained to her that I felt it was my duty as a parent to bring this to her attention. Ironically, the very next day at 10:00 a.m., the owner contacted me to mention that my daughter had unzipped another child's pants. The hurt I felt was indescribable.

But because her accusations troubled me, I sat at my desk until 3:00 p.m. with a confused look. I then told my boss that I could no longer stay. I walked off my job and never went back. Now mind you, I was still in the midst of creating my business. I still had not had a visit from Department of Children and Families (DCFS) to license my home for daycare. I was unemployed, with a house, a car and other bills and no ideal what I was going to do. I went to a temp agency and received a temporary assignment so I could be home for my children. I knew that things would be ok for the moment because I did have some funds in my 401K.

Finally, DCFS came out in October. I received my license December 17, 1996. We struggled but it was worth it. I still did not get any clients until February 1997 and was blessed to get 4 families that stayed with me for four years. The stability allowed me the opportunity to go back to school and pursued my degree in Early Childhood Development and take professional development training to run my business. Two years into my business, I met my current husband.

I have always been a determined person and I believe if you are going to do something, do it right. You must find out everything that you need to know and understand and know the rules and regulations. I always asked myself what more can I do for my clients and my business. I always wanted to offer a stimulating environment. I did not have a mentor; I did not have anyone that I could call to help when I had a difficult time with a parent. I had to learn by experience. It was always a challenge. One of my four-year parents would get upset with me at times and slam my door and go to work. I thought to myself, how could you leave your child with someone that you are so upset with? It didn't make sense to me.

Communication was very important to me as a parent and I wanted to maintain that with my clients as well. This helped me to retain my clients, obtain new clients, and sustain my business.

After being in childcare for seven years I felt that it was time for more. Again more! I decided to get my program accredited and I created a second business in connection with my daycare program.

Well, I started my second business venture; Caring & Sharing Providers' Network NFP, Inc. in January 2002. Our mission is to assist childcare providers to establish new business, professionalize existing business and to help establish and maintaining programs that will assist in running a successful child care business. CSPN is a membership organization with 21 members. We focus on "SUPREME" childcare services as well as "MEN IN CHILDCARE" advocacy. My husband and I run the daycare business together. He is my fulltime assistant and we are encouraging couples to assist each other. Without your family support it would be hard for your business to flourish. It is very important that your family has a full understanding of what your business is about so that your potential will not be limited. While having my children, my husband stayed home to run my business. He developed a new understanding about children and the sacrifices you have

Mary Smith

to make to do childcare. CSPN had a very successful first year, please pray that there are many more.

Even though, there were many painful days, I've learned a lot from everything that I've gone through. Most importantly, I learned that anything worth having is worth fighting for.

Forever in My Heart

Although I'm not their mother
I care for them each day.
I cuddle, sing and read to them
And watch them as they play.
I see each new accomplishment
I help them grow and learn,
I understand their language
I listen with concern.
They come to me for comfort,
I kiss away their tears.
they proudly show their work to me
I give the loudest cheers!
No, I'm not their mother,
But my role is just as strong.
I nurture them and keep them safe
Though maybe not for long.
I know someday the time may come
When they will have to part,
but I know each child I cared for
Is forever in my heart!

Author unknown

Bonnie Ilyse Tunick

Women In Power

Bonnie Ilyse Tunick

Fairygodmother

i wasn't born a Fairygodmother. I never really aspired to be one either. What I wanted to be was a lawyer, which I was for ten years. Also an author, which I am and always will be. But the magic happened to me one night sitting at my Dad's side, as he not so quietly passed from this world to the next. It was the most profound experience of my life. And I never have been quite the same.

I guess I had a bit of Fairygodmother in my blood.

I volunteered a great deal to bring balance into my life when I was practicing law. (I love that word "practicing;" I guess I finally got it.) I delivered meals to the homebound. I provided pro bono legal services and participated in numerous bikathons. I was on the founding board of a foundation for children facing life-threatening illness. And I became a buddy for a family battling AIDS – found another family to adopt the children, acted as power of attorney for health care, moved the family in and out of apartments and nursing homes and, finally, planned my buddy's memorial.

So my transformation to Fairygodmother wasn't as big of a jump as you'd think.

As founder and executive director of Fairygodmother Foundation, I began granting wishes from the bedroom of my condo. I drafted my life partner as my first volunteer; a childhood friend became my first board member. We drafted our mission statement over sodas in a cafeteria, laughing until we were blowing bubbles through our noses. (When you're doing serious work, you have to keep it light.) And this is how Fairygodmother Foundation was created in my father's memory to grant wishes nationally to loved ones (18 and older) facing terminal illness (having a year or less to live).

I thought it would be easy. I guess you have to be blindly optimistic to take on such a huge task as starting a charity. It also helps to be a bit insane. I led with my heart, as I always do. And I was up for the challenge, especially when certain people said I was crazy for trying or could never do it. I'd show them. I never shy away from a dare.

What I wasn't prepared for was the financial roller coaster ride. I knew my charity's mission was unique and necessary. (There are a lot of charities for sick children; few exist for dying adults.) But finding the necessary funds was excruciatingly difficult and, nearly five years later, fundraising remains my biggest challenge. With wishes flying in the door and employees to pay, I find myself tossing and turning into the night. I'd be lying if I said the stress has not taken a toll on me.

I'm the first to admit that I earned my wings the hard way. I seem to do most things that way. In this instance, I had no business plan. No money. No real expertise for doing what I set out to do. What I did have – and still do have – is a great deal of enthusiasm and commitment and empathy for families having nowhere else to turn.

When my only volunteer and I saw our first wish family off at the airport just four months after I incorporated Fairygodmother Foundation and a month before we received our non-profit status, I felt like we had won the lottery.

We put a family of seven on a plane to Disney World. The mother, a 36-year-old losing her battle against breast cancer, wanted her children to remember her laughing and smiling instead of hooked up to machines in a hospital bed. After handing the pilot a letter about our wish family, he put his pilot's cap on one of the children and gave them all a tour of his cockpit. When he upgraded the family to first class, they were wide-eyed and smiling with an air of great fortune. And they hadn't even met Mickey yet. To be giving this desperate family hope and something to dream about was the greatest feeling in the world. My heart was jumping out of my throat.

Eighteen months after working around the clock on fundraising, wish granting, administration, board development, special events, and more, the small condo I shared with my life partner began to close in on us. We were running two businesses out of a one-bedroom apartment with five phone lines and no personal space anywhere. Heading into the holidays, we found ourselves tripping over hundreds of donated toys piled high in our living room. When she finally put her foot down ("it's our relationship or Fairygodmother"), I began to seek donated office space.

I thought that was going to be easy too. Who wouldn't want to help such a deserving charity? I called nearly every church, large business, park district office, and hospital within a wide radius of my home and emerged with only one lukewarm prospect: a local hospital that might be closing its doors. I begged, tap danced, and made a pest of myself for nine months and was finally rewarded with approximately 200 square feet of donated space. I was thrilled.

At that time, I hired the charity's first employee to help me with fundraising. (I was a full-time volunteer for nearly three years.) She, too, was a novice. But at least I had some help and somebody else willing to sacrifice her health and well being for our noble cause.

With donated office space, we were able to bring in volunteers and interns to assist us. At this time, I was still doing everything from granting wishes to buying paper clips. Despite feeling hopeful because Fairygodmother Foundation was gaining momentum, I wasn't functioning on all fours. While the good news of our unique services spread, wish requests grew exponentially. Funding to grant these wishes barely trickled in. And now, besides wish expenses, I had a payroll to worry about. So I began to run up my personal credit cards. In my mind, I could continue to make sacrifices. Our wish families, on the other hand, did not have time to wait.

Although standing on shaky ground itself, the hospital let us expand into more space. I quickly filled the space with volunteers, donated travel items, donated toys, and more. I drafted a new and energized board of directors willing to roll up their sleeves and was able to attract some media attention.

A local newscaster fell in love with Fairygodmother Foundation's mission and taped a beautiful piece that aired on cable nationally. She highlighted the facts: Our charity brings peace, comfort, and lasting memories to families at the end of life. Our average wish recipient is a 40-year-old mother of two battling breast cancer, wanting to make important memories for her children before she dies. Eighty percent of our wishes involve children about to lose a parent. Our wishes are simple and varied – family trips and family reunions, transporting patients home to die in the arms of family, medical accommodations such as scooters for mobility and eye blink devices for communication, computers to stay in touch, dogs for comfort and companionship, peace gardens for memorials, and headstones for loved ones graves. And the generous reporter highlighted what I feel is the greatest statistic of all (and still is to this day): Fairygodmother Foundation has never turned away an eligible wish recipient.

Our phones rang off the walls. Everybody wanted to help. They promised to send checks, to hold fundraisers, to donate airline tickets and condo timeshares, to volunteer. And then September 11th happened. I think that's all I need to say.

We hung on for dear life. Fairygodmother Foundation continued to grant wishes and to run up my credit cards. Our board members pounded the pavement for support, and Fairygodmother Foundation was adopted by a fabulous creative design firm that gave our charity a look of quality and integrity to mirror the professionalism of the services we provide. And when I began to feel hopeful that we might climb out of the abyss created by September 11th, the economy went haywire, and we went to war with Iraq.

Today, with six employees (including myself) and wish requests flooding in far faster than funding, I toss and turn each night. I take my anti-anxiety medication. And I pray to my Dad to pull some strings in Heaven to make things better as soon as he can.

Do I regret my journey to become a Fairygodmother?

Bonnie Ilyse Tunick

No, it has made me a better person. If I knew then what I know now, would I do it again? Truthfully, I'm not sure. Okay, I guess I would. For the thousands of lives Fairygodmother Foundation has improved, I have to think the hard times are worth it. And while writing happier endings for families facing terminal illness, I have to believe I'm writing happier endings for myself and for those I love.

If I Had One Wish

If I had one wish, would I wish for great wealth, or
Would I save myself and wish for good health
Instead of short, would I wish to be tall
Instead of big would I wish to be small

Would I spend my last wish on expensive toys, or
Would I pray for safety for all girls and boys
Would I wish for an endless smile, or
Just for a friend that I haven't seen in a while

Would I wish for peace, good will to all men, or
Would I just wish for all hatred to end
Would I wish for stillness tonight
A world without wars, a world without fights

I believe if I had
But one wish to wish
I would pray to God
For more wishes to wish

By Sheila Downer

Nicole Wade

Women In Power

Nicole L. Wade

I'm A Survivor

i grew up in the 1970's on the south side of Chicago as a middle child and the only girl of four boys. My mom was a schoolteacher and my dad a Baptist minister. To begin my survivor story, I must go back to 1975 when I was 9 years old. We lived pretty comfortably and I can remember not wanting for much. I was pretty much a spoiled brat being the only girl. My mom and dad gave us younger kids everything they could afford. We had a new home, new cars, and vacationed twice a year. Christmas and birthdays were the greatest times! We did okay back then as a middle income African American family.

More than anything, I wanted to be like my mother. She was the most beautiful woman I had ever seen or known. She carried herself like an African Queen. She was independent, had her own career, her own money, and raised five children. I would get up early every morning just to watch my mom get ready for work. I wanted to spend every moment with her. She was my heroine, my best friend, and my sister. I loved her so much that I didn't want my day to begin without sharing our special time in the mornings. She would go to work while leaving us at home so our dad could get us ready for school. Since he was a big television watcher, most times he would be asleep on the couch, and I would fall asleep in their bed since I was up so early with my mother. My dad would always wake me so I could get ready with the boys. One morning, he woke me, but this morning was

Nicole L. Wade

different. He was naked while lying next to me with his hands rubbing all over my body. I felt cold because I didn't have my nightgown on anymore. He told me this was our secret, and if I told anyone, I would be in big trouble. He told me my mother would stop loving me if she knew and for the next four years my father would continue to molest me. My mom never knew what was happening because I told no one.

Dealing with four years of molestation, anger and fear, puberty, menstruation, and acne, all caused me a great deal of pain. Finally it got so bad at school that my teacher, Mrs. Thomas asked if there was anything that I needed to talk to her about. I was relieved. Finally someone could see my anger and reached out to help me. She was my angel sent from God. I was finally able to tell someone. I told her everything. In turn, Mrs. Thomas contacted my oldest brother because he was noted as the emergency contact on file. My brother and uncle came to the school to pick me up. They took me home and we all sat down to explain to my mother. At first, she was comforting and seemed understanding to everything that was said to her. But when my brother and uncle left, my mother's mood changed. She made me promised to never tell my younger brothers. She not only silenced me, but she never left my father. She thought she could protect me by securing a lock for my bedroom door and the only other precaution she took was making sure I was never alone with my dad. But how could she stay with him? How could she not protect me? Aren't parents suppose to protect their children? Well, I was still afraid, hurt and felt betrayed by my father and the only type of therapy offered was the school counselor. My mom didn't want anyone else to know. It was as if she was embarrassed of me. Why? What did I do wrong? To this day, I have never received an answer to my question.

During my senior year in high school, I finally broke down, exploding and screaming at my mom and dad one night, and my younger brothers heard everything. They were broken hearted. They couldn't believe what they were hearing. They were hurt for a lot of reasons. They felt that they had been deceived. They were also hurting because they were feeling my pain. In one night, I managed to destroy what my brothers held to be truth. They believed our father could never harm us. The burden of this night laid so heavy on me. Things became too overwhelming and I turned to drugs and alcohol.

By the time I became 18 and had graduated from high school, I had already left home. I attended a university downstate and after two years, I enrolled at Chicago State University, and moved in with my fiancé. I was married shortly thereafter and worked full time as a secretary in downtown Chicago. Because I was unable to deal with the past, my husband and I would only visit my parents during the holidays. By the time I was 21, I was a full-fledged cocaine and alcohol addict.

I knew that I had to pull myself together and it would require many sacrifices. As time past, my marriage began to suffer and after 9 years of a turbulent marriage, I divorced my husband. I endured many countless hours of counseling and drug rehabilitation. I returned to school and received my degree in Graphic Design. I landed my dream job designing with an advertising agency in Chicago and bought a four-bedroom house in the suburbs at the age of 29. I was traveling far beyond my wildest dreams, but something was missing in my life. One day I asked my Father in Heaven to reveal my mission. He sent me to a group where I spoke freely of my abuse and destructive behaviors. I met young women who had gone or were going through similar situations in their lives. My Father in Heaven told me to speak to these women and help them through the battle of turning their lives over from victim to survivor. He wanted these women to become survivors like me.

Now I tell my story to anyone who will listen. I want to motivate and inspire women who may feel life has dealt them a bad hand. If by telling my story, I inspire others to stand for the person lying dormant under their victimized skin; then I want to be that voice. I want to be that shoulder they can lean on. I want them to know they are not alone in this world, and there is help out there. There's no need for shame, anger, fear or regret. There are only life lessons and experiences, which God has made for us. He is our number one protector! He protected me during the times I thought my dad would come to me and didn't. He protected me when I thought I would lose my mind to drug abuse and keeping a secret that was eating away at my youth. I knew God was watching what I was doing to myself. Even though, I was being self destructive, He still had a plan. He was preparing me for my life's mission. I thank God for letting this author tell my survivor story.

My dad died from cancer on November 24, 1991. We did not have a relationship after I left the house in 1984. But, when I found out he was dying, I put my feelings aside and went to the hospital. As I sat by his bedside and in a calm voice, I explained to my dad the hurt and anger I had felt for so many years, which put me on the path of destruction. We talked in length and on that day I was finally able to forgive him. But most importantly, I was able to forgive myself.

Voices

She has no face...that little one
But in my mind I can see her so clearly
The wide eyes that plead with "him"...with God...with anyone
His words filled with bitterness and hate
Meant for "his" parents no doubt
But served to her on a bed of thorns
She has no voice...that little one
But I can hear her in my ears singing to herself and to the universe
A song of freedom and of someday....
"Go to your room!!! Go to your room!!!"
I hear it from the street as I walk by and I think
Yes...go to your room little one
Precious one that I cannot comfort tonight
Get into bed and cover yourself up
I will send you "my" song
And we will touch that sacred place together
Where all women who have been abused ascend to
That love that no one can take from us
The love that paints masterpieces, writes poetry and dances
Love that grows and spreads and creates more love
It is a long journey, but you are not alone
Because you cannot be separate from "us"
Your face, your voice and your tears
They are mine too
And I have made it there
I will wait for you....

By Sharon Mazanowski

Caprice Wallace

Caprice Wallace

Young, Gifted and Black.

*L*ittle black girl reared in the projects on the North side of Chicago.

- Excelled in school, one of the top in her class.

- Shipped out (of the neighborhood) to a "better" school.

- Decided to attend a "different" school.

... the Beginning of her independence. She learned a skill.

It was never easy, always tough, but I hardly noticed. I was taught that you can be/do/have whatever you want in life and have a Comforter to guide you.

I struggled. Faced racism, bigotry and nepotism. I sighed, cried, laughed and rejoiced. Fell down, got back up. But always made progress.

There were no setbacks just lessons.

- "Work 12 hours a day and we'll consider a promotion"

- "Degree first, then a promotion"

Caprice Wallace

- "Continue to work 12 hours a day and we'll pay for the degree" - A catch 22!

Moved on. Sacrificed, focused, received that mighty paper "the degree."

Ready for the "big" time. What's rightly due!

"The executive secretary position is important and it pays well."

"Oh, Degree. Oh, Computer Science. I see. The customized position should fit you well. We'll design it as we go."

More lessons learned. Growth, knowledge and experience too. I was customized!

Next up — my degreed specialty. I attained many promotions under that glass ceiling, more education and many certifications. More validated paper.

"Where's the hoop? Sure I can jump. Want to see how HIGH?"

"I can wear the Fedora today, I wore the cap yesterday."

"You realize you'll be the only woman on the team. I guess it could be good – at least the meeting discussions will be kept to the point, clean and less jokes."

"I'm not sure you can handle 1, 2, and 3 – all at the same time." As a matter of fact, I know you're not ready."

"Want to see how HIGH!"

Women In Power

Eventually, I approached burn out and realized that I was playing in a game where the players feared that I might actually WIN. It frustrated me that true recognition and capturing of the "prize" still remained elusive. What I did not know was that I was being prepared to execute His plan for me. The seed had been planted in my heart, watered with my tears, and nurtured with His love.

I was told that I was good at what I do. I made and saved lots of money for many people, filled big shoes and wore many hats. Now it was time for me to show if I believed the praise I received from others. Was it real or just flattery? Was my faith real or just wishful thinking? It was time to reach out with a purpose for His purchase. The big hat on the shelf was mine to claim - Entrepreneurship!

Many women can relate to my story. Many know it all too well and some may have not recognized it just yet. Where I came from, where I've been, where I'm going. You can be whatever you want and you CAN do it well. You must keep positive. Women face a lot of prejudice because of their gender or color. I never let that stop me because I looked pass color and gender. I see personality, characteristics and who has the power. It wasn't unusual for me to realize later, that I was the only woman sitting at the table in the boardroom. Call it naive; I call it a blessing because I never let it stop me. We must work and strive harder than the next. There are dues you have to pay but the dues become growth even if it's mastering how to deal with the situations.

Biography

Caprice Wallace is a native of Chicago and the oldest of three siblings. She earned her Computer Science degree from

Caprice Wallace

DePaul University. Caprice Wallace's venture into the competitive technology industry, has allowed her to become a rising star with various Fortune 500 companies. She often served in technical lead and project manager roles to lead critical multi-million dollar projects to success.

As a business consultant, she assists small start-ups with business plans and loan proposals. Caprice also assists emerging businesses with defining direction and finding the working capital that will either open doors or move them to the next level. Additionally, she writes grants for non-profit agencies that seek funding to support educational and awareness initiatives in an increasingly competitive and resource limited environment.

Because she is aware of what it is like not to be heard, Caprice has always been committed to giving the "silent" a voice and the tools to express themselves. She has invested a lot of her time in guiding the young people of the world. She tutored and mentored children for the Community Youth Creative Learning Experience (CYCLE), a non-profit community organization for residents of Cabrini-Green housing projects and the surrounding Near North area of Chicago. Caprice maintains her community activism by providing guidance and presentations on career development and job searching skills to young adults and seasoned job seekers. She also volunteers with the Black Data Processing Associates (BDPA) through various initiatives to build ongoing relationships with major corporations looking for talented information technology professionals.

Caprice's professional and social ventures are woven together with a common thread — To educate, empower, and encourage others so that their dreams may be realized. She is aware that when individuals feel empowered and supported the community as a whole can benefit. Whether you are an entrepreneur seeking assistance with developing your emerging business or a young person looking for your first job, Ms. Wallace will be an effective "coach" in your corner championing your cause.

Email: capwall@msn.com

Lois White

Lois White

> "Guard your heart with all diligence,
> for out of it flow the issues of life" – Proverbs 4:23

i cannot talk about victories, accomplishments and overcoming without referring to the love and boundless grace of God. I am unapologetically a Christian and this I know:

- God is real.
- His word is true, and
- His mercy endures to all generations.

In many ways, I am luckier than most. I was born into a traditional family. I had 2 parents who were there for me throughout my childhood, and both participated fully in the process of parenting (sometimes to my chagrin, as a child). I don't have any "We were so broke..." stories. Both of my parents worked, and we lived a solidly middle class life – 2 homes - basic residence and a vacation home, a housekeeper, private and parochial school education, and a college education paid for by my parents (until I got married and refused to accept money from them, since I was "grown").

The blessings in our household weren't just material. I had the great fortune of seeing first hand, how a couple in love and committed to each other lived each day. I observed how they treated each other. My father always treated my mother like he not only loved her, but treasured her. She, in turn, deeply loved, respected and treasured him.

Perhaps it was because I had so much with so little effort, that I took everything for granted. As a young woman, I was far more focused on what I wanted, than what I had. It didn't occur to me to be really grateful. The only exception to this was that after I was on my own for a while, I went to my parents and thanked them for all that they had provided. As a child, I never really appreciated what it took to keep a roof (or 2) over my head and food on the table, until I had to do it for myself.

My drama started as a young adult. At 19, I married my childhood sweetheart (no, I wasn't pregnant). But by the age of 21, we were divorced. The period following my divorce was a strange time. I felt like I didn't really "belong" or wasn't accepted anywhere. All of the sources that I would normally have gone to for consolation, were closed to me. I was castigated by family leaders, who were "scandalized" by my divorce (This type of thing didn't happen in our family, at that time). I was abandoned by many of my friends who, having finally gotten married, didn't want to associate with anyone who was divorced. The deepest hurt of all was that I was rejected by my church. The priest told me that if I dated, I would be committing adultery. Knowing that I wasn't about to live the rest of my life dedicated to the memory of a bad marriage, I sadly concluded that I was destined to go to hell. I also concluded that it was pointless to live a good life. I even thought for a while that if I was destined for hell, I might as well bust the bottom out. Fortunately for me, I don't have any criminal tendencies. The main thing that kept me "half" straight was the nagging feeling that despite what the church told me, God loved me anyway. It was the first time I considered the possibility that perhaps, the church didn't dictate who God was. It would be many years before I was to learn that God exists beyond religion and the varying opinions and theories of man.

Over the next several years, I worked and played a lot, and enjoyed doing both. My career was a series of entrepreneurial enterprises and management level positions in which I was the "youngest person," the "first black", and/or the "first black woman". After all of these years, I'm sorry to say that I'm still in such a position. I'm sorry because that fact speaks volumes to me of untapped potential; missed, and yes, denied opportunities.

Although I had achieved quite a bit professionally, my personal life was another matter. I went through a second marriage and divorce. The impact of this divorce had much less intensity. I learned, the first time around, that I could be happily single. I wasn't motivated to stay when things got difficult (and they got extremely difficult) and I already knew I could support myself. I had no clue that marriage is a covenant with God. The real damage was psychological, and perhaps because of this, it was much less perceivable. After the second divorce I concluded that although I always attract men and enjoyed their company, I had absolutely no idea how to select a "good one" for a husband.

Over this same period, I lost both of my parents. Having nothing else to "ground me" and nothing of lasting fulfillment in my life, I continued to focus on work and selected partners who were men I not only didn't love, but couldn't love. In my self-deception, this was my defense mechanism, a way of protecting my heart, while continuing to satisfy the "lust of the flesh". How many of you know that if you "sow to the flesh, you reap corruption"?

Lois White

The turning point in my life came when I realized that I was pregnant by a man that I not only didn't love, but had no incentive to marry, even for the sake of appearances. Life teaches us, through good times and bad, what we, and others, are made of. Fortunately, it does not create character; it exposes it. God, in His infinite wisdom, made pregnancy nine months for good reason. Nine months is long enough to meditate on what it means to have a child, to be a parent and be responsible and more importantly accountable, for another life. For the first time in a very long time, I thought about the quality of my spiritual life. It wasn't that I wasn't going to church; I just wasn't being "fed". I knew something was missing, so I continued to seek God.

At one point, when my child was less than a year old, things got so bad, that not only could I not see "the light at the end of the tunnel", it was so dark that I couldn't even find the sides of the tunnel. I finally realized that I knew absolutely nothing about life except that God exists and Jesus is His son. I went to God, told him this and asked him to teach me all I needed to know to be His child and a good mother to my daughter. For the first time as an adult, I became truly "teachable". It was as if a huge weight was lifted from my shoulders (it sounds trite, but it's true). Before this experience, I attributed my spiritual growth to a host of books. After this experience, I was led to read my Bible only. It was as if I was seeing it for the first time. Passages were suddenly clear and readily understandable, and I finally found the peace that I was seeking. In that period of revelation, God revealed to me that as His child, I was never alone and He reminded me that He and not my child's father, was the author of her life. As such, Angela would always be provided for. That revelation was the paradigm shift that allowed me to put in true perspective, my concerns about providing for her. Given my own upbringing, I was determined that my daughter would not be penalized because of my marital status; and I definitely rejected the popular, media notion of who and what I was supposed to be as a "single mother". Up to that time, I was sure that if her father wouldn't help with child support, life would be very difficult for us. I learned that her father is a channel, not the source of her provision. By the time he actually started paying court ordered child support, I had already begun to earn enough to provide a respectable living for her.

I have learned that all success comes from seeking God's will for every aspect of one's life. This is not the "woo-woo" experience that I would have thought it would be when I was "hanging out" in the world. God's word is not hidden. It's in the Bible and once born again, when one reads it with a heart to learn, revelation flows like a river. For me, God is no longer the far off personage who may or may not show up when I call on Him for help (which for a while, was about the only time I thought about praying). He is truly a loving father, with whom I have a personal relationship.

Today, despite circumstances that could have left me withdrawn, bitter and impoverished, I am quite the opposite. I'm attending an awesome, Word-based (scripture) church. I enjoy a career with a great company in which I've had 2 promotions in less than 2 years. I'm paid quite well. I own my own home and have a housekeeper. My daughter is beautiful, healthy, smart, accomplished in her own right, well provided for, and most importantly, a born again Christian pursuing her own relationship with God.

I am truly happy and fulfilled. I am not all that I want to be, but I know that I'm on the right path. I give God all the glory!

Lois White

One more thing... After 20 years, my first husband showed up in my life again. He's born again, spirit filled, and fervently seeking God – attributes I require in a husband. I'm not sure what will happen but I know that when God is involved, all is well . . .

"Life is a Theater" (Invite Your Audience Carefully)

Not everyone is healthy enough to have a front row seat in our lives. There are some people in your life that need to be loved from a distance. It's amazing what you can accomplish when you let go of, or at least minimize, your time with draining, negative, incompatible, not-going-anywhere relationships/ friendships. Observe the relationships around you. Pay attention. Which ones lift and which ones lean? Which ones encourage and which ones discourage? Which ones are on a path of growth uphill and which ones are going downhill? When you leave certain people do you feel better or feel worse? Which ones always have drama or don't really understand, know or appreciate you? The more you seek quality, respect, growth, peace of mind, love and truth around you, the easier it will become for you to decide who gets to sit in the front row and who should be moved to the balcony of your life. "If you cannot 'change' the people around you, change the people you're around."

Author Unknown

Robyn Williams

Women In Power

Robyn Williams

In one of his many best-selling books, Dennis Kimbro once asked the fascinating question, "What makes the great great?" I think I have the answer.

Persistence is the one dominant character trait that all successful people seem to share. Somehow, those who succeed find a way to persist in the face of failure. My fictional novels, *Preconceived Notions* and *A Twist of Fate*, have garnered me a spot on many best-sellers lists, but I know a thing or two about persisting through failure. I mortgaged my home to self-publish my first novel.

It was a struggle to get my first book published. It took four years and one mortgaged home to see my dream come to fruition. Today when people buy copies of *Preconceived Notions*, what they don't know is that originally, I had to self-publish it. I couldn't find a publishing company that was willing to publish it, so I became the editor, the typesetter, the designer, the graphic artist, the publisher, the printer, the publicist, the financier, the bookkeeper, and finally, the author all by the grace of God. I then loaded my trunk with books and literally went from door to door selling them. I'd printed several thousand copies and was fortunate enough to sell them within a six-month period of time. That gave me leverage to impress and lure larger publishing companies by convincing them that my book would do even better if published on a national level.

Robyn Williams

Like many authors before me, I learned that being picked up by a major publishing company does not necessarily guarantee success. Months after celebrating the successful second release of my first novel, the publishing company I sold my rights to folded. I was devastated because the company owed me tens of thousand of dollars in royalties that I was never able to recoup. And yet, they were still selling my books and making profits that I never saw a dime of. I felt violated and my only recourse was to sue.

It took me two years of persevering and battling the publisher, but I eventually retrieved all rights to my book. I learned so much from that experience. Mainly, that one has to do her homework on a company before signing on the dotted line. Admittedly, I was naïve and I was excited by the prospect that this well-known company wanted to publish my work. But in the end, my lack of wisdom cost me more than I could ever imagine.

I can recall the lost book opportunities. A tremendous demand had been created for my book, *Preconceived Notions*, but no one was able to purchase it because of challenges I was facing with the publishing company. The marketing dollars and public relations efforts I had personally invested in the my novel resulted in it being listed as #3 on Blackboard's Bestsellers List. It was also featured in *Essence, Emerge, Heart and Soul, Ebony*, and *Ebony Man* magazines. Actresses Angela Bassett and Vanessa Williams both said, through their agents, that *Preconceived Notions* was a "delightful" read. Filmmakers and Random House publishing company wanted to buy my rights, but my hands were tied.

Undeterred, I started work on my second novel, *A Twist of Fate*.

Published in 2000 by a different publisher, sales for my provocative sophomore efforts were phenomenal. I have high hopes that the sizzling second piece will one day be made into a blockbuster cinematic film.

In retrospect, sometimes our faith is crushed when circumstances don't turn out the way we plan. People disappoint us when their intentions prove less than honorable and sometimes we let ourselves down with our own actions. When I went through my publishing ordeal, that's pretty much how I felt for a long time. After losing so much money and potential publishing contracts, I didn't want to write anymore and I began to question myself as well as my beliefs. But I believe there's something indomitable about the human spirit. Something that shapes us and prevents us from sleeping well at night when we begin to live beneath our potential. I've been told that the true writer writes - no matter what. I had a decision to make. I could let the obstacles in my life engulf me or I could get back up and try it again.

I chose to do the latter. I chose to persist in the face of apparent failure.

Currently, I am completing my third novel, *A Fool's Paradise*, for which I believe several major publishing companies will contend to buy its rights.

Thoughts & Reflections

conclusion

Thoughts & Reflections

A *Woman In Power* is one who **creates** a new way for others. Her innovative thinking will allow her to invent a new history, a new purpose and a new idea. A *Woman In Power* is in control of her own destiny because she is neither threatened by success nor fears failure. She continues to create solutions to old and new problems while building a better world. She knows the difference between success and failure is information and never commits to anything without thinking it through first. She has a spirit of commitment and knows all too well the necessary sacrifices for greatness.

A *Woman In Power* does not wait for the approval of others – she just makes things happen. She knows that her destiny is not left up to chance and understands that setting **goals** will provide her with a better direction. She is determined and driven by her dreams because her goals are directly linked to her vision. She understands that before you can bring **change** to your future you must become uncomfortable with your present.

A *Woman In Power* is strong because of her determination and discipline. She knows that in order to **achieve** great things; you must be a great dreamer — so dream BIG.

By Sharon Taylor

conclusion

Women In Power

Emily Barr	•	President and general manager of WLS (ABC) TV
Dorothy Leavell	•	Publisher of the Chicago Crusader and Gary Crusader, was elected chairman of Amalgamated Publishers, Inc.
Michal Ann Luncsford	•	Vice president of administration of Best Imaging Solutions, Inc.
Mary G. Leary	•	President and chief executive officer
Melissa Lynn	•	Marketing coordinator
Carolyn Blanchard	•	Director of communications of Community Health Charities of Illinois
Cleo Stames	•	Vice president/ branch services
Christine R. Taylor	•	Director of education and community outreach for Ravinia Festival
Tracye E. Smith	•	Executive director for The Chicago Minority Business
Irene Natividad	•	President of Corporate Women Directors International (CWDI) and author of "Why Are There So Few Women Serving on Corporate Boards"
Jennifer Openshaw	•	Commentator on money issues for Lifetime Television and is the

conclusion

Women In Power

	• "Women & Money" columnist for CBS MarketWatch
Pamela Owens	• Senior consultant for the Terranova Consulting Group in Orinda, CA.
Oprah Winfrey	• Television Host and CEO of Harpo
Iyanla Vanzant	• Lawyer, best-selling author, and nationally recognized inspirational speaker
Corinne Wood	• Former Lieutenant Governor
Barbara Walters	• U.S. Broadcast Journalist
Jamie Foster Brown	• President of Sister 2 Sister (S2S) Magazine
Alice Walker	• Pulitzer Prize winner
Bertice Berry	• Sociologist, educator, television personality, bestselling author. Acclaimed nationally as a keynote speaker, lecturer, inspirational speaker, and motivator.
Nikki Giovanni	• One of America's hottest and most controversial poets. An African-American woman, lover, and feminist.
Senator Carol-Mosley Braun	• United States Senator
Linda Johnson-Rice	• President and Chief operating officer of Johnson Publishing Co.

conclusion

Women In Power

	based in Chicago.
Hillary Rodham Clinton	• Senator
Dr. Ruth J. Simmons	• President of Brown University
Dr. Maya Angelou	• Poet, educator, historian, best-selling author, actress, playwright, civil-rights activist, producer and director
Eddie Bernice Johnson	• Congresswoman
Dr. Mae Jemison	• Astronaut, scientist, humanitarian, orbit aboard the space shuttle Endeavour, September 12, 1992, the first woman of color to go into space.
Mayor Shirley Franklin (Atlanta)	• 58th Mayor - City of Atlanta
Ann Fudge	• Former president of Kraft Foods' $5 billion Beverages, Desserts and Post Division
Marion Jones	• First female track and field athlete to win five medals at a single Olympics in Sydney
Yolanda Adams	• Gospel Music Artist
Gloria Steinem	• Feminist
Sandra Day O'Connor	• Associate Justice United States Supreme Court
Dr. Ruth J. Simmons	• Ruth J. Simmons named 18th

conclusion

Women In Power

	president of Brown University
Sandra B. Parks	• President and CEO of The Daily Blossom
Bonnie G. Hill	• President of B. Hill Enterprises, a consulting firm in Los Angeles that specializes in corporate governance and board organizational and public policy issues.
Reatha Clark King	• Ph.D., president and executive director of the General Mills Foundation.
Barbara L. Bowles	• Chairman and CEO, the Kenwood Group, an equity investment advisory firm based in Chicago.
Gwendolyn S. King	• President of Podium Prose, a speaker's bureau/speech-writing service in Washington, D.C.
Dorothy Terrell	• Senior vice president of worldwide sales for NMS Communications and president of the Boston-area company's Services Group, sits on the boards of General Mills Inc., Sears, Roebuck & Co. and Herman Miller Inc.
Sandra Austin Crayton	• Chairperson of the family-owned Lake Eufaula Ford Mercury Inc. in Eufaula, Ala.

conclusion

Women In Power

Johnnetta B. Cole	• Ph.D., president emerita of Spelman College who recently retired from her professorship post at Emory University in Atlanta, sits on the boards of Coca-Cola Enterprises and Merck & Co.
Brenda J. Lauderback	• Retired president of wholesale and retail for Nine West Corp.
Debra L. Lee	• President and chief operating office of Black Entertainment Television in Washington D.C, sits on the boards of Eastman Kodak Co. and WGL Holding (Washington Gas & Light Co.)
Paula A. Sneed	• Group vice president and president of E-Commerce and Marketing Services, Kraft Foods, sits on the boards of Hercules Inc. And Airgas Inc.
Joyce M. Roch	• President and chief executive officer of Girls Incorporated, serves on the boards of Anheuser-Busch Cost. And SBC Communications Inc.
Hazel R. O'Leary	• Chief operating officer of Blaylock & Partners, a New York investment banking firm, sits on the boards of UAL (the parent company of United Airlines) and

conclusion

Women In Power

	AES Corp. (a power development company).
Lois D. Rice	• Guest scholar at the Brookings Institution in Washington, D.C.
Mellody Hobson	• President of Ariel Capital Management, Inc., a Chicago-based investment management firm specializing in equities, with more than $7.8 billion in assets under management.
Dr. Wanda M. Austin	• Is senior vice president of the engineering and technology group at The Aerospace Corporation, the principal engineering resource for the national's military space program, based in El Segundo, California.
Cathy Roos	• Vice president of corporate financial planning for Federal Express, the world's largest express transportation company.
Helen Gurley Brown	• Editor in Chief of Cosmopolitan magazine.
Carla Harris	• Head of Equity Private Placement, Morgan Stanley
Kim Crawford	• VP and GM of Networking Dell Computer

Resources

conclusion

Resources

Books (Entrepreneurship)

1. Ready or Not ... Get Set Go (An Entrepreneur's Guide to Startiing and Maintaining a Successful Business) by Sheila Taylor-Downer

2. Start Your Own Business: The Only Start-Up Book You'll Ever Need by Rieva Lesonsky (Editor)

3. Small Business For Dummies® by Eric Tyson, Jim Schell

4. Successful Business Planning in 30 Days: A Stepby-Step Guide for Writing a Business Plan and Starting Your Own Business by Peter J. Patsula

5. The Small Business Handbook: A Comprehensive Guide to Starting and Running Your Own Business by Irving Burstiner

6. Black Enterprise Guide to Starting Your Own Business (Black Enterprise Series) by Wendy Harris, Wendy Beech

7. Innovation and Entrepreneurship by Peter F. Drucker;

Change (Personally & Professionally)

1. Leading Change - John P. Kotter on What Leaders Really Do (Harvard Business Review Book)

2. The 7 Habits of Highly Effective People by Stephen R. Covey

conclusion

3. The Life Strategies Workbook: Exercises and Self-Tests to Help You Change Your Life by Phillip C. McGraw

4. What color is your parachute - A Practical Manual for Job-Hunters and Career by Richard Nelson Bolles

5. Who Moved My Cheese? An Amazing Way to Deal with Change in Your Work and in Your Life by Spencer Johnson, Kenneth H. Blanchard

6. The Road to Optimism: Change Your Language-Change Your Life by J. Mitchell Perry, et al

Self-Improvement

1. What You Can Change... and What You Can't: The Complete Guide to Successful Self-Improvement: Learning to Accept Who You Are by Martin P. Seligman, Martin E. P. Seligman

2. Twelve Steps to Self-Improvement: A Crisp Assessment Profile by Elwood S. Chapman, et al

3. Move Your Stuff, Change Your Life: How to Use Feng Shui to Get Love, Money, Respect, and Happiness by Karen Rauch Carter

Stress

1. Don't Sweat the Small Stuff for Women : Simple and Practical Ways to Do What Matters Most and Find Time for You by Kristine Carlson, Richard Carlson

conclusion

2. The Relaxation & Stress Reduction Workbook by Martha Davis, Matthew, Ph.D. McKay, Elizabeth Robbins Eshelman

3. A Survival Guide to the Stress of Organizational Change by Price Pritchett, Ron Pound

4. Peterson's Stress Concentration Factors, 2nd Edition by Walter D. Pilkey, Rudolph Earl

5. Stress Concentration factor by Peterson, Joel E. Peterson (Contributor), Karin M. Clark (Contributor)

Spiritual Growth

1. Until Today! Daily Devotions for Spiritual Growth and Peace of Mind -by Iyanla Vanzant

2. There's a Spiritual Solution to Every Problem by Wayne W. Dyer

3. 10 Secrets for Success and Inner Peace by Wayne W. Dyer

Mentoring

1. Coaching and Mentoring for Dummies by Marty Brounstein

2. Beyond the Myths and Magic of Mentoring: How to Facilitate an Effective Mentoring Process, Revised Edition by Margo Murray

3. Co-Active Coaching: New Skills for Coaching People Toward Success in Work and Life by Laura Whitworth, et al

conclusion

4. Leader As Coach: Strategies for Coaching & Developing Others by David B. Peterson, Mary Dee Hicks

5. Women Mentoring Women: Ways to Start, Maintain, and Expand a Biblical Women's Ministry by Vickie Kraft

Inspirational

1. The Prayer of Jabez: Breaking Through to the Blessed Life

2. The Hope Chest by Condy Jacobs (Editor), Leslyn Museh (Compiler), Cindy Jacobs (Editor), Leslyn Musch (Compiler)

3. God's Words of Life for Leaders by Zondervan

Investing

1. Rich Dad, Poor Dad: What the Rich Teach Their Kids About Money--That the Poor and Middle Class Do Not! by Robert T. Kiyosaki, Sharon L. Lechter (Contributor)

2. Investing For Dummies® by Eric Tyson

3. The Wall Street Journal Guide to Understanding Money & Investing by Kenneth M. Morris, et al

4. Being Right or Making Money by Ned Davis

Organizations

1. Count Me In for Women's Economic Independence
   22 West 26th Street, Suite 9H, New York, NY 10010, Call us! (212) 691-6380, www.count-me-in.org, E-mail - info@count-me-in.org

conclusion

Non-profit organization raises money from women to be loaned to women. Provides education, micro loans, and business training scholarships.

2. **National Association for Women Business Owners (NAWBO)**
   NAWBO Headquarters
   1411 K Street, N.W., Suite 1300, Washington, D.C. 20005
   Telephone: (202) 347-8686, Fax: (202) 347-4130
   E-Mail: national@nawbo.org, www.nawbo.org

It is the only national chapter based membership organization for women business owners. It offers its members strength in public policy action, networking opportunities, significant money saving benefits and opportunity to expand business revenues.

NAWBO Information Service Line
1-800-55-NAWBO (1-800-556-2926)

3. **National Foundation for Women Business Owners (NFWBO)**
   1411 K Street, NW, Suite 1350, Washington, DC 20005-3407
   Phone: 202-638-3060, Fax: 202-638-3064
   e-mail: info@nfwbo.org, www.nfwbo.org

A non-profit research foundation, NFWBO's mission is to support the growth of women business owners and their organizations through gathering and sharing knowledge. It is the premier source of information on women business owners and their firms worldwide.

Source of information and statistics on women business owners and their businesses providing non-profit research, leadership development and entrepreneurial training.

conclusion

4. **Women's Business Development Center**
   8 South Michigan, Suite 400, Chicago, IL 60603
   Telephone: (312) 853-3477, Fax: (312) 853-0145
   www.wbdc.org, E-Mail: wbdc@wbdc.org

   Founded in 1986, the Women's Business Development Center has earned a national reputation for quality, comprehensive and responsive programming and support for prospective, emerging and established women business owners. The WBDC delivers vital information on all aspects of business ownership: Entrepreneurial Training, Individualized Business Counseling, Financial Assistance, Procurement Assistance, Women's Business Enterprise Certification, Targeted initiatives in youth entrepreneurship, Child Care Businesses, Welfare-to-Self-Employment, Advocacy

5. **The Commonwealth Institute**
   69 Newbury St., 5th fl, Boston, MA 02116, Tel: (617) 859-0080, Fax: (617) 262-3777,
   www.commonwealthinstitute.org,
   E-mail: mhalvorsen@commonwealthinstitute.org

   Commonwealth Institute helps women entrepreneurs grow their businesses through peer mentoring, networking, and exposure.

6. **American Woman's Economic Development Corporation (AWED)**
   216 E. 45th Street, 10th Floor, New York, NY 10017, 917-368-6100 or email AWED at info@awed.org, www.awed.org

   Provides business training, counseling, and support to aspiring women business owners.

conclusion

Mentoring & Networking

7. **American Business Women's Association (ABWA)**
   9100 Ward Parkway, PO Box 8728
   Kansas City, MO 64114-0728 USA
   Phone 800-228-0007, Fax (816) 361-4991
   E mail: abwa@abwahq.org, www.abwa.org

   The mission of ABWA is to bring together businesswomen of diverse occupations and to provide opportunities for them to help themselves and others grow personally and professionally through leadership, education, networking support and national recognition.

8. **Women In Sports Careers Foundation (WISC)**
   (714) 848-1201 - phone
   (714) 848-5111 - fax
   wiscfoundation@aol.com
   A member-based organization dedicated to supporting women in sports related careers. Online career center includes job listings, sports rolodex, networking chat rooms, career support, events, etc.

9. **National Organization for Women**
   1000 16th Street, NW, Suite 700
   Washington, D.C. 20036
   (202) 331-0066

10. **National Association for Female Executives (NAFE)**
    (publishes Executive Female magazine)
    127 West 24th Street
    New York, NY 10011
    (212) 645-0770

conclusion

11. National Coalition of 100 Black Women

The NCBW mission is the development of socially conscious female leaders who are committed to furthering equity and empowerment for women of color in the society-at-large, improving the environment of their neighborhoods, rebuilding their communities and enhancing the quality of public and private resources for the growth and development of disadvantaged youths. NCBW is dedicated to community service, the creation of wealth for social change, the enhancement of career opportunities for women of color through networking and strategically designed programs and the empowerment of women of color to meet their diverse needs.